MW01031150

Bite into this one,
Jenn. It's for
people who give
a damn.

w/aloha

Randy

NICARAGUA STORY

Back Roads of the Contra War

W. M. Raebeck

"Nicaragua Story—Back Roads of the Contra War" ©
Copyright 2022 Hula Cat Press
all rights reserved

Cover design by W. M. Raebeck
front cover photos by W. M. Raebeck
back cover photos depict Augusto Sandino & Michel Sauriol
    (photographers unknown, but appreciated)

No part of this book may be copied, reproduced, or used in any
way without express permission from Hula Cat Press or the author.

Library of Congress Control Number: 2022908033

ISBN 978-1-938691-18-8

At least 20% of the proceeds from "Nicaragua Story—
Back Roads of the Contra War" goes directly to protecting wilderness,
wildlife, all creatures, and oceans from human violation, insensitivity, and
ignorance.

This book is sourced from a responsibly managed North American forest,
meeting the requirements of the Independent Sustainable Forestry
Initiative Program.®

Visit 'WendyRaebeck.com' for other books by W. M. Raebeck, photos,
news, author appearances, and to receive her newsletter.

PO Box 510058
Kealia, Hi 96751
HulaCatPress@gmail.com

To the people of Nicaragua

who stayed

Acknowledgments

I respectfully acknowledge the many hundreds, probably thousands, of volunteers (*internationalistas*) and brigade workers (*brigadistas*) who flocked to Nicaragua to support her idealistic vision during the Contra War. The mental and physical muscle lent by these civilians enriched Nicaragua's spirit and morale, proving the world WAS watching and that the United States government's agenda wasn't the final or global word. These volunteers put their home lives on hold for months, occasionally years, to perform the broad array of tasks they'd enlisted for. Their presence in Nicaragua also created an unforgettable community of international solidarity.

I'm ever grateful to Michel Sauriol, who shared the discovery, passions, and joys of Nicaragua, and who helped me immeasurably in the heat, discomfort, frustration, and disillusion of those back roads. A man of ideals and purpose, Michel was forever game, courageous, kind, and strong. Since this story's focus is on Nicaragua, not personal relationships, his character may seem somewhat down-played. Suffice it to say, he was a loyal, resilient companion on a tumultuous expedition.

To hold this story up so long after it was written, it had to be underpinned with scaffolding, in the form of political back-story. Marcie Powers, Donna Carsten, and Anndrias Hardisty helped me do that, and I sincerely thank them.

Back in 2015, Marcie was first to read the story and sold me on footnotes. A few years later, Donna helped track down decades-old mainstream newspaper articles illustrating what the American public was being told during that era. Then, once some history was introduced, Anndrias checked it over.

But even after supplying background (that, unfortunately, I knew little about when I was in Nicaragua), this story wasn't done. Books in progress sometimes steal the reins from the author and start to transform almost by themselves. Just as I thought I'd entered the home stretch, I looked into *older* Nicaraguan history—from long before the Contra War—that revealed how burned by the U.S. Nicaragua had been...for eons.

That earlier history massively impacted the decades to follow. And I wondered how deep to delve...bad enough my book was about war, but now history, too? But the book was having its way and all I could do was type along behind. Adding more icky politics would take finessing, but it had to be done—there was more to the story.

All's fair in love and war. So I've doggedly pared down my findings into the most presentable form possible.

Notes

Fear not, this isn't a dense political treatment, but an unusual, often moving, firsthand account. The bulk of the text is my original Nicaragua journal, penned while down there and tagged with actual dates and locations of each entry.

❧

Why this story is so important to me is because war never seems to go away. Nor do disagreements, misunderstandings, lies, and deceit....in every aspect of life, including family, government, and media. Therefore, sadly and ironically, this story stays current though it took place in the mid 1980s.

❧

Because so few today know about or can recall details of the Contra War, *italicized* notes are embedded throughout the story to demystify the politics, the region, the history, and the players. In most instances, these are inserted straight into the narrative, not placed at chapter's end—this seemed more reader-friendly. Despite any slight interruption to flow, *please don't skip or skim over the notes*, even if you abhor history or detest politics! The footnotes complete the story. Here, again, I strived to minimize and smoothly weave in the info. (You'll find the second half of the book almost footnote-free.)

Know that each *italicized* note is a direct quote from the source identified above or beneath it, but I've dispensed with quotation marks around whole footnotes. I've used quotation marks only for quotes within that quote. It's cleaner this way. (But you'll find a few diversions from the format.) If no source is attached to a footnote, then it's me offering more detail, hopefully of interest.

However, any thesis-writers, researchers, and Ph. D's out there may justifiably critique my footnote style! I took a little creative license. But I think my system works best for this unique tour de force.

❧

To ground you on your journey, maps of Nicaragua, Central America, and Mexico are provided. They're rather crude, but most locations mentioned in the book can be spotted. And, at the end of the book, are English and Spanish glossaries to assist with foreign and unfamiliar words and terms. I think you'll find these beneficial.

Just to clarify the geography, Central America is the isthmus connecting North America to South America. This north/south chain of seven fairly small countries veers slightly east and west. The countries are Guatemala, Honduras, Nicaragua, Costa Rica, and Panama, with the smaller nations of Belize to the Caribbean side and El Salvador to the Pacific side. Mexico is not part of Central America.

❧

Throughout this book, all mention of 'soldiers' refers to Sandinista soldiers, unless stated that they are the Contra.

Now, one small caveat before we begin, (and you can handle it): fairly early in the book is a brief historic overview. It's as compelling and appalling as it is educational and relevant. Digest it as best you can, to deepen your understanding of Nicaragua and her people. (I only wish I'd known more of this history when I was down there.)

Finally...I want to assure you that even though this 'memoir' or 'adventure book' or 'travel book' is a departure from those genres—in that you go to war, and you think about history—I promise that when you finish this book, you'll know far more about not just Nicaragua but the United States.

Okay, ready to hit the road?

Disclaimer

This is a people's story about the struggles of a nation. Politics were wildly at play. Yes, they are part of the book; yes, I had a political bent in solidarity with the Sandinistas. But let's not align yesterday's views with today's madhouse of ideologies—we're turning back the clock. You'll get more from the story, and feel more, if you temporarily suspend any biases (from then or now), even your pet ones. This book depicts a moment in time as lived by a freelance journalist seeking the 'truth.'

Her biases, too, were challenged....

~ WMR

Mexico and Central America

Central America

Nicaragua

"The history of liberty is a history
of resistance."

~ Woodrow Wilson

NICARAGUA STORY

Back Roads of the Contra War

Table of Contents

Preface

How I Got Involved

In 1985, as a freelance journalist, I covered the Central American Peace March ('*La Marcha por La Paz*') from Costa Rica to Mexico City, for the *LA Weekly*.

A Costa Rican bus dropped me at Nicaragua's southern border. Though not wildly surprised there was no public bus into Nicaraugua from there, particularly at 5 p.m., I hadn't expected no traffic at all. But who enters a remote outpost of a war-torn country after sundown?

Before I could envision a worst-case scenario under a mean moon, two Dutch journalists in a Jeep plucked me from the roadside. Dirk and Yon, who later became friends, were brilliant company for the three-hour ride to the capital of Managua. Having been based in Nicaragua two years, they gave me the run-down on 'gringos in solidarity.'

Then, the following day, I caught up with the marchers in the village of Estelí, up near Nicaragua's northern border.

The purpose of the March, attended by activists from dozens of countries, was to oppose covert wars in Central America, oppose America's duplicity and corruption pertaining to these wars, and oppose any country meddling in the affairs of another. All the news that the marchers had read back home, about the deadly conflicts in Guatemala, El Salvador, and Nicaragua, incensed them. And, since trusted intel through mainstream media was impossible to obtain, a solidarity march through the entire region seemed a means of bringing worldwide attention to the whole travesty.

Few of the marchers had intimately studied the three Central American wars one by one, viewing them more as overall violent and unfair aggressions perpetrated by the same bully. But as the March advanced northward, now about to cross Nicaragua's border on foot into Honduras (a country with established ties to Washington), the procession was refused entry. Honduran soldiers several rows thick vowed to continue blocking the border day and night, keeping the peace march OUT. No Commie sympathizers comin' in here.

At a non-negotiable halt suddenly, the March found itself detained in Nicaragua. It would have to deliberate how to somehow get over, under, around, or through Honduras, a country stretching from Caribbean to Pacific. (The map illustrates how few options the Peace March had for circumventing Honduras.)

Though El Salvador was accessible to the west by crossing the treacherous Gulf of Fonseca (in canoes of hollowed-out logs, purported to be terrifying), that country had the bloodiest, dirtiest covert war of all. Salvadorans were continually *desaparecidas* (disappeared), and the March had earlier determined El Salvador too dangerous to protest in or even travel through. (Though

I only spent one day there myself, the stealthy black cars everywhere with darkened windows and the unmarked planes touching down and taking off suggested covert *everything*.)

So, being barred from Honduras wasn't just a roadblock for the March, it was a setback. Numerous factors were involved in strategizing a next move....

As the marchers pondered options, hoping the Hondurans would just relax, the days became weeks, and the weeks added up to a full month. But Honduras held firm, armed soldiers rooted at the border—this united nations of protesters was *unwelcome*.

However, as the March held meetings all day every day (hearing from every single participant, ad nauseum), all of us—marchers and journalists—found ourselves witness to the extraordinary plight of Nicaragua.

As the Contra War was raining down social upheaval, this small country's commitment to autonomy, and the strength and spirit of its humble populace were a blindside for all of us. We hadn't known how long Nicaraguan citizens had craved the most basic human rights and fair governance. And now, finally, they were getting it. Their new leaders, the Sandinistas, had made them a promise...and were delivering on it.

I'd never experienced actual revolution—aside from idealistic hippie days, John Lennon style. Sure, the spirit of revolution had been pitched my whole life as part of the U.S. Constitution, the American way, but to see it taking place, without commercialism, consumerism, or even capitalism, made it undeniably clear how corrupt the U.S. had become, Constitution or not, Bill of Rights or not.

The ideals and intentions of Nicaragua were contagious and compelling, if not highly unusual and tragically unlikely.

Possibly *because of* the U.S. Constitution and Bill of Rights, something was sparked in me — gut-wrenching conviction about freedom and human rights. Involuntarily, I was swept headlong into the country's passion, captivated by an idealism you could actually see, smell, and taste, idealism you could feel in your blood.

It's hard to deny that depth of feeling. And counterintuitive to try. So, as a journalist (*periodista*), I felt empowered, duty-bound even, to advance the truth about the creepy Contra War — a polar-opposite perspective down here on 'the front' than that spun by mainstream media in *Norteamerica*.

After four long weeks — Honduras unflinching and marchers frustrated — the March settled on a plan. It would divide up, each participant choosing his or her own route around Honduras — either by plane, or by sea and land through the Gulf of Fonseca to El Salvador (at their own risk). Non-Americans might try to breach that northern border and cross Honduras, luckier perhaps without the March. One way or another, all would then re-convene next week in San Cristobol de las Casas, a small city in southern Mexico, not far from the Guatemalan border.

Good luck to all. God Speed!

Needing to cover the March to its final stop,
Mexico City, I chose to jump a flight to Guatemala City,
then bus my way north through Guatemala, then on into
southern Mexico.

But…I'd contracted the fever, and was motivated
to somehow return to Nicaragua. Soon. To support the
world example this tiny country was setting, against crazy
odds. [1 & 2]

1) How the Peace March came about:

*In January 1983, to prevent a U.S. inva-
sion of Nicaragua, and any region-wide conflict that might follow, the leaders of Panama,
Mexico, Colombia, and Venezuela (countries
bordering Central America) decided to promote
a Latin American alternative to President Reagan's Contra War against Nicaragua. Calling
themselves the Contadora group, after the Pan-
amanian island where they met, these countries were soon joined by four South American
nations—Brazil, Peru, Uruguay, and Argentina
(called the Lima Support Group). These eight
countries united to build a regional peace plan.
They named it the Contadora process, and it
was hailed around the world.*

2) from The Christian Science Monitor, Oct. 26, 1984:

*But Honduras, El Salvador, and Costa Rica
(Central American countries heavily backed by*

the U.S., financially and militarily) now say extensive changes are required before they would accept the Contadora plan.

Several U.S. and Central American diplomats and analysts said these three countries' objections came after a short but intensive lobbying effort by the Reagan administration.

During this stall in the peace process, 'La Marcha por La Paz' was conceived, to support the Contadora process by means of a six-week trek from Panama City to Mexico City—directly through the three countries stalling the plan.

Part One – The Mission

~ 1 ~

Peace March with Benefits

The lay-over in Nicaragua proffered more than revolutionary fervor. For a couple of us, there was an unexpected twist....

Also covering the March, was a jovial five-person film crew, also from LA, that I instantly befriended. Discussing March logistics and sharing political data flooding in, we'd dine together and all stay in whatever *hospedaje* (hostel) someone had been tipped off about. Another appendage of the March was a three-man film crew from Montreal, who, by sheer proximity as well as simpatico mindsets, naturally linked up with our LA gang. This mobile band of nine made up the full media attached to the March.

Along the route of the March (completed largely by bus, with scheduled protest stops on foot), the marchers lodged at schools or churches where they'd prearranged shelter. But we free-range *periodistas* (journalists and filmmakers), with our separate roles, found our own accommodations.

And, while the March debated how to pole-vault Honduras, there was little for us to document. So, holed up back in Managua with unstructured time, we'd work on our stories, fiddle with equipment, study Spanish, absorb history in the making, and interview the phenomenal cross-section of activists down here in solidarity (such as original members of the Abraham Lincoln Brigade from pre-World War II). [3]

As we *periodistas* co-mingled in a hostel those final days in Managua, I casually began taking note of one of the Canadian filmmakers. The more I observed how he resonated with Nicaragua's situation and what we were all doing, the cuter he grew.

It wasn't until our last evening that I realized he was also taking note of me.

We then fell into each other's arms.

But the next day, the Montreal crew had to set out across Honduras in their Dodge Dart. (Canadians welcome there, just no Yanks.) Where, when, and how the doughty documentarians would rejoin the March, should they survive Honduras, was not known.

Since I was poised to hopscotch Honduras over to Guatemala City, they dropped me at Managua airport on their way back up to the border.

But Michel and I had fallen for each other. And thus was set our date with destiny.

> ~ *January 14, 1986, in flight,*
> *Managua to Guatemala City*

3) Members of the Abraham Lincoln Brigade—American civilians who volunteered in the Spanish Civil War in the 1930s—about whom I knew zip until I interviewed them in Managua—were in total solidarity with the Sandinistas. Seeing undeniable parallels between the Spanish Civil War and this Contra debacle, they felt they had no choice but to mobilize all over again. Young when they went to Spain, and now in their 70s and 80s, the Lincoln Brigade (celebrating its 50th anniversary) had the same conviction again that had propelled them to Spain. My article about these extraordinary men is reprinted in this book's epilogue.

No Pasaran

I bolted a Flor de Caña rum and Coke
as the departure line grew smaller
bartender wanted twenty cents for it
I wanted to cut myself some slack
leaving Nicaragua wasn't what I had in mind

But, last one out, I had to go
my turn to walk out the door
I hadn't had time to think about it
working to the last split second

A hundred feet across the tarmac
big white plane was swallowing everyone
crescent moon lit the scented night
"No pasaran," I said to the soldier at the gate
("They will not pass")

He smiled

I had twenty more steps of Nicaragua
Nicaragua, I breathed her in
Nicaragua, I don't want to leave
Nicaragua, my eyes filled with tears

~ *January 14, 1986, in flight,*
Managua to Guatemala City

Central Mexico was a long way and three countries from where Michel and I had said adios. And when the Canadians didn't reappear as everyone else regrouped in southern Mexico, the entire assembly grew concerned about the threesome and their dodgy Dart. Nobody trusted Honduras and few marchers had ventured through there.[4] But third world travel by car is sketchy by definition, and those Canadians were tough and competent enough.

> 4) *Because of its central location on the drug-smuggling route, much of the cocaine bound for the United States either comes from or passes through Honduras. With drug traffic comes violence and corruption. The Honduran murder rate is among the highest in the world.*
>
> — *"What is a Banana Republic? Definition and Examples," by Robert Longley, 'ThoughtCo,' Dec. 6, 2021, ('ThoughtCo.com/banana-republic-definition-4776041')*

A week later, the last day of the March in Mexico City, there were the Canadians, suddenly in our midst again. Turned out they'd had a rash of car troubles and couldn't catch the swiftly moving March powering north through Mexico to make up for lost time.

Though Michel and I were eager to be together again—not to mention Mexico City was a fun change of scenery and we'd been working for weeks—the marchers had now fulfilled their mission and were all scrambling back to the distant lives they'd abandoned. And the Canadians, too, still had the Northern Mexico desert to negotiate in that bad-ass buggy, plus the USA to cross from south to north.

I had charted my next move by then, also. I'd return to LA via the Baja Peninsula on public buses. Hey, what's another 1500 miles? One of the LA film crew amigos was a willing companion. But he needed to get going....

So, after just one more night together, Michel and I again kissed goodbye.

~ 2 ~

Passionate Plans

Back in Venice, California, I stayed in gear. My heart was in Nicaragua.

I had found the leaders of the revolution curiously down to earth. Nicaragua's struggle rang of authenticity and energy. The presidential motorcade was four black Jeeps, with President Daniel Ortega[5] driving one of them. The ambiance down there felt like maybe the New York underground of the late 1950s—there was a beat. Succinct images, like that Jeep quartet rounding corners in the capital, symbolized a looser power, something our own grand-scale conditioning couldn't fathom.

There was purity of purpose. It was Hemingway. It was blood—life and death co-existed. Even the lack of commodities drove people to fight harder; everything was on the line. Like a collection agency in the U.S. taking the car, the couch, and the kids—when it's down to the kids we'll do anything. In Nicaragua, it was down to the kids.

Here, we only fight to maintain our ease. Nothing's at stake. Nicaragua's passion had power and depth

Americans don't find even in cinemas. But that stark simplicity, that life or death, *must* become known to us... *because it's our war, too.*

But right now, at this moment, no one here feels a thing....

Down there, souls are being tried. Nicaragua faces its opposition butt-naked. And new ways to stay strong are shared like hip jargon is shared up here.

~ Venice, California, April 24, 1986

> 5) *José Daniel Ortega Saavedra, born November 11, 1945, was the leader of Nicaragua from 1979 to 1990, first as Coordinator of the National Reconstruction (1979–1985), then as president (1985–1990). A leader in the Sandinista National Liberation Front (FSLN or 'Frente Sandinista de Liberacion Nacional'—the government's official name), his policies implemented leftist reforms across Nicaragua. As of spring 2022, and continuously since 2007, Daniel Ortega has served again as president, with his wife Rosa Morillo as Vice President. Their two children also hold government positions.*

I'd spend the next six months home in Venice, integrating with like-minded others and attempting to secure journalist and photography assignments to cover expenses for a return to Nicaragua. Then I'd head back down to publish real news, not propaganda. Knowing that phenomenal community of rugged *internationalis-tas* was there bolstered my certainty that I needed to be part of this.

∽ৡ৴

Both of us smitten, it wasn't long before Michel came to California.

With our Nicaragua concerns front and center, we confabulated about traveling back there together. I was going no matter what, but he felt he, too, could scare up some film work or journalism and join me. There wasn't much time, though — pressing issues weren't letting up, the war was continuing.

We agreed to drive down in my VW camper as soon as the summer heat abated in the deserts we had to traverse. Selecting an early September departure date, all we still had to do was line up work.

Though Michel's native tongue was French Canadian, his English was fairly fluent and his aptitude for language generally impressive. So we weren't feeling any barriers; the relationship was groovin' along.

In fact, so enthralled with each other were we that we decided to get hitched while he was in my longitude. Both in our early 30's, it was a swell time to pair up. And, though lover-boy had had no intention of ever marrying, he wanted to make an exception just this once. I assumed he'd also appreciate the green card he'd qualify for, but he was repulsed at the mere thought. Apparently Nicaraguans weren't the only ones sickened by most of what the U.S. stood for. "I have no interest in ever being American," said Michel through acid reflux.

Being 1986, few in our generation were big on marriage or even lasting relationships. So a Sin City wedding, decided upon the day before, was par for the course. Off to Vegas we drove, five merry friends of mine forming the wedding caravan.

In the following months, we newlyweds made an East Coast sweep to meet each other's clans—mine on Long Island, Michel's in Montreal—then, sadly, it was phone time again until our Latin love could percolate south of the border.

I began pitching stories to newspapers and preparing the camper. Said vehicle, patiently waiting for just this caliber of adventure, was equipped with everything we'd ever need. Plus, having a car in Nicaragua would be pure gold. And, even though wars vexed our trail, not only had we both already been down there and both knew Spanish, but Michel was an automotive genius and generally fearless.

Eventually landing two assignments from the *LA Weekly*, two from *The Village Voice* in New York, and one from the *Easy Reader*, a weekly paper in Hermosa Beach, I was good to go. And *galvanized*. The op was in high gear now, no major hindrances…except that dear Michel hadn't lined up any jobs yet. But he was phoning it in pretty convincingly.

That was…until he broke his arm in a bicycle accident.

Then everything ground to a halt on his end. He'd need surgery, then healing time....

Of course I felt terrible for the poor hubby. And he was miserable about holding things up.

However...by then, my preparations were several paces ahead of his. A sub-letter was scheduled to move into my apartment, and all my personal effects and cargo were packed into the camper. I was set to scram; had just been waiting for the green light from the spouse...the one with the broken arm in Montreal and no jobs in Nicaragua.

What now?

Then, just a few days later, everything was further incinerated when I went to retrieve something from the camper, parked on the street a few blocks away, to find it had been broken into and *everything* of value was gone.

The double-whammy of losing both everything and everyone necessary for the launch was a head-in-hands blow. I now had no cameras, no electronic typewriter (pre-computer days), no rechargers, not even my leather jacket or boots, and...no companion. Everything critical to the production was up in smoke.

What the heck kind of cosmic injunction was this? The momentous undertaking not meant to be? Too dangerous, too expensive, too out there? Were we being foolhardy? "The universe must have major misgivings...."

But, sometimes when the universe conspires to block you, that's the moment to flip it the bird, throw a grenade into the blockage, and declare war on fate. "Universe, we need to talk."

Setbacks can make great springboards.

Two good friends each lent me a camera, so again I had one for color and one for black and white. I bought a new electronic typewriter, a better one. Now I just had to tell Michel to heal up and meet me in Managua as soon as he felt up to it.

"Sorry, Universe, this means too much to put aside or wait around with fingers crossed." I had to get going. Otherwise everything was about to evaporate. Plus I had work commitments now and my apartment was sublet!

But was I to drive 1500 miles alone in a vintage van through five countries, four deserts, and three wars? I admit to batting the option around…. But, no. I parked my camper in a friend's driveway, bought a plane ticket to Nicaragua, and bid my sub-letter adieu.

Bummer Michel and I wouldn't have a vehicle down there now (if he ever showed), but so much for plans…. It had all seemed too smooth anyway. Other people may do things with planning, foresight, and supportive cohorts, but flying by the seat of the pants had always been my default travel mode.

~ 3 ~

Butterflies

My stomach arrived first in Nicaragua. Butter-flies. I half-expected Daniel Ortega to meet me at the gate.

Preparing to de-plane, I'd chatted breezily to a few American men who were (obviously) not getting off in Nicaragua. Then, at the first customs stop inside the terminal, an American lady, arriving to spend a year working for a health organization, told me she'd heard a snippet of conversation while passing those guys on the plane. "Betcha that blonde's a real rabble-rouser," they'd said.

"They were talking about you," she laughed. "What had you said to them?"

"Nothing," I said. "It must've been the look in my eye. Or maybe they noticed that I started taking deep breaths of Nicaraguan air as soon as we landed."

Observing that the taxi fare from the airport had quadrupled since I was last here eight months ago, I arrived at the Santos. This *hospedaje* (hostel) was packed like before and I was lucky to secure one of five beds in a newly converted chamber that had been the family living room last time.

The *Señora* remembers me, and when I'm signing
in says she remembers my heirloom ring, too. I ask if she
remembers the three French Canadians with the malfunc-
tioning car, and she's not sure. I tell her anyway that I fell
in love with one of them in that hammock over there and
now we're married. "No wonder you came back to this
hostel," she says, but can't compute why hub's in Canada
while wife arrives *solita* in Nicaragua. She's reassured
when I say he'll be here in three weeks.

The Santos is a shocking dump. By fluorescent
glow, it borders on the macabre. I'm glad now I didn't
persuade any pals to accompany me on this venture. A
dumpster-diver in the U.S. would wince at this furniture,
these hammocks, that broom over there. If I'd first arrived here by night, I wouldn't have checked in. Fortunately, I remember the color of the morning sky, the palm
shadows dancing across the courtyard, the skin tempera-
ture of the light winds, and the reason why everything's a
mess.

~ *September 12, 1986, Managua*

It's all coming back to me, a storm of sensations.
What I loved: the thick tropic air, the dirty little children,
the friendly Sandinista soldiers, the oddness of being here
at all. And what I didn't like: the rudeness of the staff at
the Intercontinental Hotel (posh establishment where we
foreigners buy newspapers); the 'bourgeoisie,' chubby
and tasteless in their sunglasses; and the 6 a.m. cacophony of voices, radios, motors, animals, and hammering.

It's changed, too. Not only are the wooden armchairs of the *hospedaje* now painted orange, not only has
the hardworking couple replaced the handmade staircase
with a crooked concrete flight, and put potted plants in
the outdoor lounge, not only has the exchange rate doubled making everything more expensive, but the street
life seems different, too. In my research back in the
States, the Nicaraguan situation struck me as more black
and white than it seems here today. Walking along the
streets, I feel disconnected from the politics, wanting to
ask every person where they stand, their thoughts about
the war, the struggle....

I ran into a lady I remember, of the bourgeoisie—a blatantly identifiable class in Nicaragua, not trusted by the Sandinistas—who lives in a corner house and
stops tourists to offer them black market rates for dollars. She hustled me for twenty minutes, that I permitted
to see what might be revealed. We ended up two houses
down at her sister's where she then tried to rent me a
room. I didn't like her face or her pitch and didn't sell
her any dollars. What I wanted to ask her, but couldn't,
was, "Are you a Contra?" [6]

6) *In Nicaragua, the political definition
of a 'Contra' is anyone supporting the armed opposition to the elected Sandinista government now
ruling the country.*

What I'm uncomfortable with, out in the streets,
is that my position is obvious. Simply being a *gringa* in
Nicaragua indicates I support the Sandinistas—why else

would I be here? *There's a war on.* Yet there's no way to determine, unless you ask, where a Nicaraguan stands. So, until my Spanish gets refreshed, locals are always going to know my stance but I won't know theirs.

❧

Managua, the capital, is in the western portion of the country. Today, I was itching to get out to other areas, but undecided where to. Allegedly, a cattle car to Leon (to the northwest) was leaving at 6 p.m. for the reasonable fare of 50 *cordobas* ($.02). But since it arrives by night, I shelved that thrill 'til maybe after Michel gets here.

I strolled over to the Intercontinental instead, to sit in the sedate lobby and consume the Sandinistas' daily news, aided by my Spanish dictionary. In adjacent straw armchairs, two Americans were chatting. One introduced himself to the other as a Fulbright scholar studying Nicaraguan poetry. The other was with the Architects and Planners Brigade up in Matagalpa (south-central Nicaragua). Hearing that, I had to interrupt to ask if he knew Steven, Phoebe, and Jeff (LA friends of mine with the same organization).

Of course he did. In fact, this guy Tom then said he was leaving pronto for a meeting in Matagalpa and would I like a ride up there? I accepted readily, looking forward to hearing about the organization's activities as we motored along. Tom had only two hours to get to the meeting, though, so I've never packed or left a place as swiftly as I did the Santos—to which I'll soon return, and where I left half my gear.

We then sped off in the Toyota truck Phoebe had spoken so fondly of. (A vehicle means everything in Nicaragua.) [7]

7) *Architects and Planners in Support of Nicaragua has just completed an 8-month construction project of 23 houses (so far) and a school in the remote hills of central Nicaragua. They're now heading back for more, despite impending escalation of the war.*

The site for the next 25 houses is a tiny community called Momanal, a cattle cooperative boasting 83 residents and 800 head of cattle. Though Contra battles have recently occurred as close as 8 kilometers from Momanal, the brigade has developed a loyalty to and concern for the community. Because Momanal residents have seen the 23 homes built nearby, the brigade has credibility. And the Architects and Planners have met twice with community members to work on improving the homes' design. In addition to smoke-free stoves, kitchens will now be separated from the general living area. (Lung disease from smoke inhalation accounts for a large percentage of deaths among Nicaraguan women.)

The Americans will also plant gardens to counteract the food shortage and upgrade the local diet. "There are hardly any beans left," report brigade workers. "Nicaraguans are surviving solely on rice and tortillas."

The Trade Embargo, imposed on Nicaragua by the American government last spring, hasn't made things easier for American work brigades though. "The Embargo isn't only aimed at trade with Nicaragua," said Jeff Bishop, one of the group's founders, "but also at support groups like ours. By spelling out what can be sent down and what can't, the Embargo allows stuff for the Contras but not for others. This forces groups like ours to go through a third country like Mexico, Canada, or Sweden to get supplies through. Shipping vast amounts of building materials from a third country entails tremendous difficulty and extra cost."

The Architects and Planners brigade faces increasing danger, too, because, it is said, the Contras are no longer sparing internacionalistas. Plus, the situation, if anything, is worsening. "There are so many isolated areas in Nicaragua," says Phoebe Hirsch, a teacher and volunteer co-ordinator in both LA and Nicaragua. "More than 50 percent of the population lives in such regions. And isolation is what the Contras take advantage of."

All the same, another brigade is shaping up, and both Jeff and Phoebe will soon be departing for 6 more months in Nicaragua.

When asked if they experience any opposition to what they're doing, the answer is no. Then Phoebe says, "Unless you mean all the

*networks, every major newspaper across the
country, and the U.S. government—there's that
opposition."*

  *— consolidated from two of my own articles:
  L.A. Weekly, August 15, 1986, &
  The L.A. Reader, May 12, 1986
  "Architects and Planners heads for Pancasan"*

∽☙∾

Tom's been down here three months, arranging
a technical assistance branch of the organization. With
colloquialized Spanish and the intention of staying two
years—barring an American invasion, or possibly even
during one, whatever that would entail—he's living in
Matagalpa and meeting government officials to determine the most valuable/feasible projects for American
volunteers in the region.

Tearing through the *barrios* (residential neighborhoods) outside Managua, then extricating ourselves from
the maze of the *Mercado Oriental* (the Eastern Market),
we embarked on a thirty-kilometer discussion about
gringos as revolutionaries, reasons for coming here, reasons for staying...one of those exchanges during which
strangers become friends. Careening along the lush, peo-
pled road through hills and villages, horses, carts, and
farm stands selling watermelons, with hot wind gushing
through the cab of the truck, the passion of the revolution came rushing back to me.

Matagalpa has a lost-in-time quality. In the late afternoon glow, with surrounding hillocks haloed in shimmering green, it's all pastels. It has angles and prettiness that the flatter towns up north, like Estelí and Somoto (where I previously spent time), do not. And, in keeping with Nicaragua's overall unspoiledness, Matagalpa's not uglied by chintzy new structures.

Settling into a small hotel, I was dirty from the road, wet from the rain, and my clothes had that clean-dirty smell that allows a couple more days' wear. Emptying my pockets onto the rickety table, I pulled out three batteries, three pens, an army knife, and a wad of money. Ah, my durable old self again, free-range and fully charged.

But, unlike the ambiance outside, my hotel cell reads more like Charles Dickens—ancient ochre walls, brown fingerprints, and cobwebs. What would make a nice wooden floor happens to be the ceiling. And below, were it light enough to see, there might be a red terracotta floor. The thin plywood wall doesn't reach the ceiling, so I'm privy to every breath of a next-room conversation between a mother and child. But the bed has a pillow, something the Santos lacked.

Rain is applauding outside, an ovation for the last hour. And though I'm actually prepared for this season, in my haste today, I left my poncho in Managua.

So, when the showers eased up, I proceeded along the cobbled streets to a nearby hang where sweet tooths from far corners of the globe converge and talk politics between spoonfuls of sundaes, while wagon-loads of soldiers rumble through the streets.

Up here, troops are more suited up, more on alert. Closer to the front, they're more implicated than those in Managua, though substantial numbers fill both towns. The inevitability of this place is heartbreaking. Meanwhile, a soldier on guard outside plays catch with the little boys.

☙❧

Driving up here, Tom and I had swapped Contra stories (Tom's) and Reagan stories (mine).

His news was heavy. Sixty kilometers east of here is a settlement called Mulukuku where about 400 *campesinos* (country folk, farmers) have been relocated into new houses. Several days ago, at 1 a.m., the Contras attacked. Three from the village were killed — an elderly man and a seventeen-year-old girl were victims of rocket bombs hurled into their home, and an eight-year-old girl was seized, decapitated, and left on the ground.

Tom learned this from a female soldier friend who'd been ten kilometers away from Mulukuku at the time. Her troop was summoned in by radio after the attack. Arriving there after a two-hour hike through the jungle by night, the soldiers felt sickened at the sight of the child's corpse. Tom said his friend had returned to Matagalpa highly emotional and speaking of revenge.

There's no question that things have intensified. I'm writing at a turning point in this revolution. On one hand, the Nicaraguans have already swallowed a lot — years and years of armed attacks. On the other, if Reagan has his way, the worst is yet to come. An American invasion, with all the sophisticated warfare imaginable, is a veritable possibility.

According to resident foreign journalists, the U.S. is not likely to launch an offensive until after the November elections Stateside, after the voting's done. But one thing's certain, this war isn't winding down. [8]

~ September 13, 1986, Matagalpa

8) The Senate soon will debate on President Reagan's request for $100 million in aid to the Contras fighting the Sandinista government in Nicaragua. In June, the House ended two years of opposition to Contra aid by narrowly approving the President's proposal, so the Senate's deliberations will be the last opportunity for full debate before a major escalation of U.S. involvement.

— NY Times, OpEd, August 8, 1986

Part Two – Some Back Story

~ 4 ~

Regional Summary

When it comes to war, one can never dig too deeply for the truth. But, knowing what went down earlier, one can better grasp how today's conflict evolved. A cursory overview of regional 20th century history goes something like this: [9]

> 9) Some events in this chapter are drawn from
> "The Nicaraguan Revolution: the Somoza Regime
> and Sandinistas" ('study.com,' Jan. 22, 2015).

Central America was plagued by revolution and war for much of the 20th century, partly because the U.S. voiced uber-concern about keeping communism out of the Western Hemisphere. But, from the early 1900s, more forceful entities were at work—financially motivated American corporations grabbing resources in 'banana republics' (as tropical third-world nations were condescendingly labeled by the U.S.). [10, 11, 12, & 13]

10) *"Banana Republic" has become a derogatory term used to describe a corrupt, self-serving dictatorship that solicits and takes bribes from foreign corporations for the right to exploit large-scale agricultural operations—like banana plantations.*

...During the early 1900s, multinational American corporations, sometimes aided by the U.S. government, such as United Fruit, took advantage of depressed economies dependent on only a few export crops, and built banana republics in Central American countries such as Honduras and Guatemala.

...The American-owned company would orchestrate a successful coup d'etat that replaced the elected government with a military government, then install a local dictator friendly to foreign business.

...United Fruit soon became the sole employer of the Honduran people. So complete was the company's control of Honduran agriculture, transportion, communication, and political infrastructure that the people called the United Fruit Company "El Pulpo"—The Octpus.

— *"What is a Banana Republic? Definition and Examples," by Robert Longley, 'ThoughtCo,' Dec. 6, 2021, ('ThoughtCo.com/banana-republic-definition-4776041')*

11) *In 1917, even before World War I, a secret U.S. governmental envoy was sent to Costa Rica, Nicaragua, and Panama to enlist the support of leaders there. Heading the envoy was Foster Dulles, nephew*

of Secretary of State, Robert (Bert) Lansing. Dulles was also a lead lawyer with the powerful firm of Sullivan and Cromwell.

Sullivan and Cromwell—a mammoth law firm for America's largest corporations—had already played a key role in building the Panama Canal and in creating the Republic of Panama (previously part of Columbia). And after literally starting a new country, the firm then named itself offical legal council for Panama.

12) In the 1930s, Sullivan and Cromwell grew to be the largest law firm in the United States. "Even calling it a law firm," it was written, "is missing the point. It's a strategic nexus of international finance, the operating core of a web of relationships that constitutes power."

11, 12) – from: "The Brothers—John Foster Dulles, Allen Dulles, and Their Secret World War," by Stephen Kinzer

13) When Colombia wouldn't give Cromwell the deal he wanted for the canal, that's when he orchestrated the break-up of Colombian territory. Setting up his own railroad in Panama, he then used those employees to launch a coup. Then, after the coup, the railroad employees became government workers inside the new Panama. And money would be sent down from New York to give huge cash bribes to pay off all the local supporters.

> *Cromwell believed his greatest project was*
> *the creation of the Panama Canal and, with it,*
> *the new country of Panama. ...And this stuff is*
> *still going on; Sullivan and Cromwell is still the*
> *most powerful corporate law firm on Wall Street.*
> *The same people that Sullivan and Cromwell were*
> *defending 100 years ago are the same people that*
> *screwed everybody over during the crash of 2008.*
>
> — *from "Sullivan and Cromwell: Capitalism,*
> *Intelligence, and Fascism," interview with*
> *Hugo Turner ('Our Hidden History.org')*

First stop on the secret envoy of 1917 was Costa Rica, ruled by brutal dictator General Federico Tinoco. (Tinoco had seized power in a coup promoted by the United Fruit Company, a Sullivan and Cromwell client.) But Foster Dulles found 'a willing partner' in Tinoco, who was deeply in debt to United Fruit, and Foster urged Uncle Bert's State Department to reward Tinoco's 'sincere friendliness' by recognizing his government. (However, President Wilson took a dimmer view of generals who deposed democratic governments, and rejected the proposal.) [14]

> 14) *Latin America wasn't the first region*
> *Dulles played a role in. In Cuba, he'd already*
> *quelled a backlash against a U.S.-backed right-*
> *wing election. And that first foreign interven-*
> *tion showed him how easy it can be for a rich*
> *and powerful country, guided by its wealthiest*

corporations, to impose its will on a poor and weak one.

> — *from: "The Brothers—John Foster Dulles, Allen Dulles, and Their Secret World War," by Stephen Kinzer*

Next country on the mission was Nicaragua. There, the U.S. had already engineered the overthrow of a liberal regime when it had tried to borrow money from European banks rather than Sullivan and Cromwell's American bank client. The U.S. had then assisted into power General Emiliano Chamorro, a pliant dictator in whom Foster found another friend—who borrowed from the American bank.

Back in D.C., Uncle Bert knew precisely how the dots were connected and, of course, that Sullivan and Cromwell was the law firm for the new government of Panama. Yet despite screaming conflicts of interest, and his own family ties, he still appointed his nephew, Sullivan and Cromwell lawyer Dulles, for this Central American envoy. Though this fell squarely under 'abuse of power' in the most flagrant, even criminal, sense, such modus operandi by the United States rolled on unceasingly until......well, we don't really have an end date.

Foster Dulles, his brother Allen, and one or two other power moguls were laying a foundation and national credo that would long endure. [15]

15) *Before there was a CIA, the corporations carried out their own coups, and Sullivan*

*and Cromwell was the firm you'd go to if you want-
ed that kind of thing done. The United Fruit Company was another corporation that could carry out
coups on its own.*

> *— from "Sullivan and Cromwell: Capitalism,
> Intelligence, and Fascism," interview with
> Hugo Turner ('Our Hidden History.org')*

*16) Then…by the end of Harry Truman's term,
the CIA had been granted an expanded role as an advocate of covert operations, willing to go beyond what it
had done before, even overthrowing governments.*

> *— from: "The Brothers—John Foster Dulles,
> Allen Dulles, and Their Secret World War,"
> by Stephen Kinzer*

*17) …The CIA basically took over the covert
operations that Sullivan and Cromwell or the United
Fruit Company used to do on their own. And, ever
since then, we've lived in this CIA-controlled America. Now you have this one agency that carries out
coups all over the world on behalf of corporate America. And built right into the government. And paid
for with public money.*

*…People now know the Dulles brothers were
to blame for all of it, but it's crucial to see that Eisenhower was totally in on all of it, as was Nixon.*

*…During the Eisenhower administration
(after Truman), Nixon was Vice President, Foster*

Dulles Secretary of State, and Allen Dulles Director of the CIA. They all worked closely together and were into all the secret operations, the CIA stuff.

...And a number of members of the Eisenhower administration had ties to United Fruit (from stock-holders, to positions on its Board of Directors, to relatives in the company). In fact, no American company has ever been so well connected to the White House as United Fruit during the Eisenhower administration. ...Even the President's personal secretary Ann Whitman was married to United Fruit's publicity director Ed Whitman.

— from "Sullivan and Cromwell: Capitalism, Intelligence, and Fascism," interview with Hugo Turner ('Our Hidden History.org')

Justification

"No nation can reach the position of a world power, as we have done, without becoming entangled in almost every quarter of the globe, in one way or another," was Foster's view,[18] about which he boldly wrote and spoke throughout his lengthy political career, often underscored with religious fervor.

18) According to Foster Dulles, "There are two kinds of people in the world. There are those who are Christians and support free enterprise, then there are the others."

— from "Sullivan and Cromwell: Capitalism, Intelligence, and Fascism," interview with Hugo Turner ('Our Hidden History.org,')

It was said in Washington, "When Foster Dulles started talking about 'America's priceless spiritual heritage,' or 'the hopes of all who love freedom,' lesser nations had reason to become uneasy." [19]

20) The Sullivan and Cromwell of Foster and Allen Dulles (both attorneys for the firm before they became Secretary of State and Director of the CIA, respectively) sought nothing less than to shape the affairs of all the world, for the benefit and well-being of the select, their clients. "Forcing other countries to accept trade arrangements favorable to American business interests will ultimately benefit everyone," they asserted.

But Senator Taft of Ohio, running for president in 1948, rejected the idea that destiny was calling Americans to over-spread the globe. "That is based on the theory that we know more about what is good for the world than the world itself," he repeated in speeches. "It assumes we are always right and anyone who disagrees with us is wrong. Other people don't like to be dominated. And we would then be in the same position of suppressing rebellions by force as the British were during the 19th century." [20]

19-20) — from: "The Brothers—John Foster Dulles, Allen Dulles, and Their Secret World War," by Stephen Kinzer

But, unwavering, the Dulles brothers practiced what they preached — relentlessly, and held tremendous sway for decades. But their global maneuvers were never intended to benefit 'everyone.' Over time, leaders of those obliging, dictatorial, third-world regimes became extremely powerful, wealthy, and formidable…while the common people stayed dirt poor. [21]

21) — from: "The Brothers—John Foster Dulles,
Allen Dulles, and Their Secret World War"
by Stephen Kinzer

Nicaragua under Somoza

The Dulles brand of capitalist imperialism was as pronounced in Nicaragua as anywhere else.

Beginning in 1922, America opposed Nicaragua's then-President Jose Zelaya because he wanted to work with Japan in building a canal across Nicaragua that would rival the U.S.-controlled Panama Canal. Though a century old, the Monroe Doctrine of 1823 held that the U.S. has sole dominion over the Western Hemisphere and the right to intervene in any country therein "to prevent influence of other nations." This doctrine has remained a guiding, often convenient, force for U.S. policy in this hemisphere. European nations, in particular, may not grab territories over here. But nowere does the doctrine state that Western Hemisphere nations 'belong' to the U.S.

Ousting Jose Zelaya, the U.S. backed a succession of Nicaraguan presidents to its liking (held up al-

ways by the brutal Nicaraguan National Guard), who
gave the U.S. and U.S. companies significant control
over Nicaragua's treasury, finances, and railroad. Eventually, the U.S. ushered in the cold-blooded Anastasio
Somoza, along with his followers, the Somozistas. And
the Somoza family would control Nicaragua for decades.

But under the stunning atrocities and inequities of
Somoza, a populist (people's) resistance began to grow
under a Nicaraguan named Augusto Sandino.[22] Sandino
wanted not only justice but North American influence
out of Nicaragua.

*22) Sandino was one of the most import-
ant and successful guerrilla fighters of the 20th
century, literally driving the US Marines out of
Nicaragua against nearly impossible odds.*

*...Sandino was not an intellectual and he
was not a Marxist. Nor was he a revolutionary
by training or by study. He was a mechanic from
near the small town of Massaya, Nicaragua. ***

* Augusto Sandino is pictured on this book's back cover.

*— from: "The Mouse Kills the Cat: Augusto
Cesar Sandino's Rebellion against the US,"
by Daniel Kovalik
('The Internationlist 360,' Feb. 21, 2022)*

So the people revolted. And a civil war broke out.
And the U.S. withdrew the Marines in 1924...but
only to send in an even greater Marine invasion in 1925.

That's when Augusto Sandino took the lead of hundreds of mostly peasant guerrillas to repel the assault.

Sandino and his troops persisted for YEARS, despite unthinkable hardship, and actually drove the Marines out of Nicaragua in 1933. [23]

> *23) Sandino and his forces proved a formidable power which could neither be caught nor vanquished. ...His small, ragged army fought for years against 12,000 US invaders and the ferocious Nicaraguan National Guard.*
>
> *— from: "The Mouse Kills the Cat: Augusto Cesar Sandino's Rebellion against the US," by Daniel Kovalik ('The Internationlist 360,' Feb. 21, 2022)*

After extensive guerrilla warfare—that no one ever anticipated from the clever and well-supported Sandino—American forces, only through deception, helped Somoza defeat him. [24]

> *24) Shoring up the National Guard under the leadership of Somoza ("a son of a bitch, but our son of a bitch," according to Franklin Roosevelt), Somoza lured Sandino to Managua under the premise of a peace deal, then assassinated him Feb. 21, 1934.*
>
> *Somoza, backed by the US, then declared himself president of Nicaragua and quickly re-*

pressed Sandino's followers and supporters…. And Somoza, his son, then his grandson, ruled Nicaragua with an iron fist for the next 45 years. (Until the FSLN finally ousted them in 1979.)

— *from: "The Mouse Kills the Cat: Augusto Cesar Sandino's Rebellion against the US," by Daniel Kovalik ('The Internationlist 360,' Feb. 21, 2022)*

With Sandino gone and the U.S. a solid ally, anyone against the Somoza regime was destroyed. Historical accounts disclose economic deprivation, cruelty, and murder.

The Sandinistas

Under the oppression of the Somozas, and after Sandino's assassination, seeds of true rebellion took root in Nicaragua's impoverished people. The resistance began to organize and, in time, the common people formed their own political party based on fairness and equality. Calling themselves 'Sandinistas,' after Augusto Sandino, their party was named the FSLN or *'Frente Sandinista de Liberacion Nacional'* (the 'Sandinista National Liberation Front').

Accordingly, Anastasio Somoza was assassinated in 1956.

But…his sons replaced him. And their rule was marked by the same repression and ruthlessness. With its U.S. backing, the Somoza regime endured. In fact, in

1959, the U.S. became even more overt and generous in bolstering Latin American governments it had helped establish.

But the people's uprising in Nicaragua continued throughout the 1960s. The Sandinistas wanted, most of all, self-determination. Not communism, not capitalism — just their own constitution and their own future.

In 1972, Nicaragua was devastated by an earthquake. And when foreign aid from all over the globe began flowing in to help the victims, the Somoza regime, still in power, withheld that money from the populace, keeping it for themselves. It was then the Somoza family began losing favor in the eyes of the world. Everyone now became aware of the Sandinistas, and approved of what they saw. With the poverty-stricken population united behind them, the FSLN, at long last, began weakening the Somoza regime. The tide was turning. [25]

> 25) ...But the Somozas didn't leave without a fight. In the end, 50,000 Nicaraguans died, 100,000 were wounded, 40,000 were orphaned, and 150,000 became refugees, almost entirely through the aerial bombings of Nicaraguan cities, reminiscent of US bombings there in the 1920s and 1930s—all this to ensure that huge swaths of the country would remain in ruin for years to come.
>
> — from: 'The Mouse Kills the Cat: Augusto Cesar Sandino's Rebellion against the US," by Daniel Kovalik ('The Internationlist 360,' Feb. 21, 2022)

The Contra War 26 & 27

*26) In the ten years prior to the final over-
throw of the Somoza regime in 1979, all the U.S.
television networks, combined, devoted exactly
one hour to Nicaragua—that hour exclusively on
the 1972 Managua earthquake. And in the eighteen years from 1960 through 1978, the New York
Times had a total of three editorials about Nicaragua, a country of no concern as long as the Somozistas' tyrannical rule wasn't challenged.*

*When that rule was challenged by the
Sandinistas in the 1970s, the U.S. tried to insti-
tute "Somozismo without Somoza"—the same corrupt system but with someone else as figurehead.
When that didn't work, President Carter tried
maintaining Somoza's National Guard as the
base for U.S. power there.*

*Punishingly hard and sadistic always, by June
1979, the Guard was bombing residential neighborhoods in Managua, carrying out massive atrocities
against the Sandinistas, and killing tens of thousands of people. Yet the U.S. ambassador down there
told the White House it would be ill-advised to call
off the bombing since the U.S. policy was to empow-
er the Guard to keep the Sandinistas down.*

*— from: "What Uncle Sam Really Wants,"
"The Contra War in Nicaragua"
by Noam Chomsky, 2002*

And everyone knows who supplied the planes and bombs.

27) But the U.S. ambassador to the Organization of American States (OAS) wouldn't let the bombing continue. And a few days later, the Somoza family bailed to Miami with what was left of the Nicaraguan national treasury. The Guard collapsed, and the Carter administration evacuated the Guard commanders out of the country in planes with Red Cross markings (a war crime).

— from: "What Uncle Sam Really Wants," by Noam Chomsky, 2002

❧

It's imperative to recognize the historical landmark of the Sandinistas winning control of the country (by fair election). After all the Nicaraguan people had been through, at long last they had a free country.

And once the Somozas fled for their lives and were out of the picture, and there were no obedient dictators for Uncle Sam to operate through or hide behind, the U.S. had no footing there. Nicaragua was its own country, under elected leadership. And, after fighting to the death for their freedom for fifty years, the Sandinistas weren't about to give it up now! But they knew their adversary well; and remained armed and prepared to die.

So now, if the U.S. had a problem with the Sandinistas, it would have to declare some official issue. But not even sharing a border or having any credible grievance against Nicaragua, what possible banana could Uncle Sam peel with this pesky little republic?

So, as it happened...NO official issue was ever addressed, no diplomacy attempted, no aggression ever authorized by Congress. Yet an actual war against Nicaragua was waged all the same. [28]

> *28) The U.S. began reassembling the Guard on Nicaragua's borders, renaming them "Contras" or "Freedom Fighters." And these fighters would soon become the mercenaries Ronald Reagan used to launch a large-scale terrorist war against Nicaragua, combined with economic warfare, by means of embargo, that was even more lethal. (Plus, the U.S. strong-armed other countries to not send aid to Nicaragua either.)*
>
> *— from: "What Uncle Sam Really Wants," by Noam Chomsky, 2002*

Hence, aside from one small nation taking on the world's mightiest super-power, the Sandinista government had to also immediately seek and establish new trade agreements, since all the U.S. imports they'd relied on were snatched away by an all-inclusive trade embargo.

Part Three — Conversations

~ 5 ~

The Sad Truth

A jovial, barefooted grandma in a pink dress beckoned me into this cafe, pleasant perch to read the paper cover to cover, my daily homework for learning the language and staying abreast. Endless green hills roll right from this open door, beside which I'm drinking coffee, shooing flies, and scooping out the daring few. Ten feet away, an eight-day-old boy is being bathed, to his dismay, in the kitchen sink. After dunking him, the old lady washes her hair in the same sink, scrubbing her face afterwards with her long tresses in lieu of a wash-cloth. Young men wander freely through, few ordering anything; perhaps they're relations.

Instead of accepting my restaurant offer last night, Tom suggested dinner at his place because his house-mate, Don, was supposedly cooking up a vat of something. They reside in a large, new, government house built for locals and *internationalistas* working in Matagalpa.

After four years in Nicaragua as an electrical technician, Don has lost all semblance of being North American. And having just recovered from hepatitis, he's lost weight, too, and is blue around the gums. In his standard *campesino* garb of baggy pants and cowboy hat, it was impossible to decipher who he'd been in the States.

Food prep lasted an hour and a half, during which we conversed about this region in relation to the war. As the rice cooked, Don brought out his AK-47 for me to look at. He never got past showing me how to aim though, because the rifle was so heavy, conversation kept drifting, and then, to my relief, it was time to fry the onions.

As we settled at the table, six other members of the household stomped in from the night, sobriety of war enveloping them. In army uniforms, belts, and boots, they carried rifles and seemed to shake off where they'd been as they thumped into the room.

Nicaraguan government housing planners, they were returning from several days up at Mulukuku, where the recent attack was. And, especially at night, no one travels these Contra-ridden hills without the cold fear of death. Ambush and road mines are the greatest threats, and far more frequent after sundown when warning signs can't be observed. These guys said at one point along the way they'd seen several men in olive green scrambling away from the roadside as their vehicle approached. Sandinistas wouldn't do that. They stopped their Jeep where the men had been spotted, but no one was any longer in sight.

As a gesture of concern and support for Mulukuku's terrorized residents, these soldiers had been sent there to research options for helping out with more housing and a generator. But Don and Tom disagreed with that sort of assignment; and after four years in these parts, Don, at least, understands how things work. He said the farmers up there see these clean, city people in their wrist watches and uniforms as fakes, people flirting with danger for sport, and that a few more 'official' people showing up at a time like this means little.

After washing up, most of the men went out, two off to Managua. One stayed with us at the table though, a smallish guy with a beautiful face and all-seeing black eyes. For the next hour, he probed us about what became of the '60s hippie ideals in the U.S. — love, peace, back to the garden, disdain for corporate greed. "Is it not still alive in some respect?" he wanted to know. "If not, why not?"

We three Americans took a ponderous inhale.

"Is there no hope of change from the civilians of the U.S.?" the guy pressed. "If not, why not?" He sincerely wanted to understand what has happened in the States. "What about Jesse Jackson? Is there hope there?"

Our answers made him sad. Us, too.

The Vietnam War, we said, was stopped by students who didn't want to be drafted, at a time of peaking economy when idealism was affordable — especially ¹ young people (students) with older people's (⸱ material backing. When the war ended ⸳ pretty much did, too. Students grew as adulthood set in. Credit cards arrived, then sprang the yuppies—ex-hippies with debt. And today's students, we said, are in debt from the get-go, so ideals are secondary to them.

"But what happened to all the hippies?" the soldier implored, unable to believe such conviction could…dry up. There wasn't accusation in his questions, but, like us, he just felt incredulous that such a strong movement could…peter out, or utterly fail.

Meanwhile, Nicaragua now desperately needed people like the hippies—had maybe even counted on them helping stop Reagan's agenda…. Surely, we three open-minded Americans could shed light on what had changed.

This question, that I'd asked myself a thousand times, brought tears to my eyes.

We three looked at each other for what to say…. "Well, everybody grew up and…."

The young man watched our eyes—our answers might quell his bewilderment. We attempted to respond, while also trying to sort it out for ourselves.

No one ever talked about this in the United States; everyone had just gradually pivoted somehow. Up there, the hippie movement seemed to now be chalked up to just another beautiful, possibly immature, vision—despite all it had meant to our generation, our country, and the future. So it took a long moment to find words. It was crushing to acknowledge that such a movement, cherished and unshakable as anything any of us had ever believed in, had run dry, or worse…had been…a fad.

And it was gut-wrenching to have to admit, "You know, in American culture, ultimately, there are few real binding idealistic issues of the heart. Or so it seems to be evolving. Americans have 'things' in common.... In the American way," we stammered in a kind of brutal confession, "even the ex-hippies are now involved in protecting and keeping what they have. Material things have a meaning in the U.S. that's impossible to understand here. Materialism is a way of life."

~ September 16, 1986, Matagalpa

29) excerpt from 'Broken,' The Easy Reader,
by Wendy Raebeck, Mar. 17, 1988:

...Actress Corinne Bohrer, who lives in Venice, recently returned from a delegation donating medical supplies to Nicaragua. "I didn't need to go to Nicaragua to see wounds and the faces of the children," she said. "I already knew what was going on. But I realize now that underneath my 'intellectual awareness' was hiding this little blonde girl waving a tiny American flag—'I'm an American, I'm a good guy. My daddy was a handsome Marine.'

"Last week I was in Nicaragua and...I don't know...I just have never felt so shamed. The faces of the children, they got to me. I shoved the little flag-waving girl out of a helicopter.

"It's not about gory stories and bloody photos, but about those other casualties of war: truth and context. I've been lied to. How can they say those things about Freedom Fighters? How can Ronald Reagan say 90% of Central Americans live under democracy so we have to help the Freedom Fighters save that last 10% from Communism? After seeing what I saw, it really got me."

Cathy and Marv Treiger, health practitioners from Santa Monica, went to Nicaragua last November with a health organization. "In the hospital," said Cathy, "we saw a lot of people who'd lost limbs in the war. It really touched me that people who'd lost limbs had no animosity toward the American people, even though it's our government that manufactures and plants these bombs through the Contras. When I came back, I was depressed for about two weeks. I think it was because...." She couldn't find the words.

Cathy then remembered an image, and said, "The night we got back, we turned on the TV and the first thing we saw was a commercial of a guy and a girl. He turned to her and said, 'Your palace or mine?' I mean, the people of Nicaragua don't have enough to eat, not enough medical supplies, and no parts for machines."

...Paul Astin, a UCLA student of Public Health in Latin America, was on the same health delegation. He was introducing Nicaragua to a *homemade oral rehydration solution for preventing death from diarrhea. "One of the main causes of death among children in the third world is diarrhea," he said. "Breast milk, out of fashion, (Nestle and other formula companies try to associate bottle-feeding with higher status), is replaced by infant formula, using local water supplies usually contaminated. Unsterilized bottles can grow bacteria, so bottle-feeding can cause diarrhea in infants. And diarrhea can kill an infant in a matter of hours, especially in the tropics. In 1978 in Nicaragua, diarrhea was the main cause of death in children under five. But the revolution overhauled the health system, focusing on prevention, and by 1983 diarrhea was lowered to the fourth cause of death in young children. Now it's back up."*

In 1985, on the main highway into Managua, was a giant billboard depicting a mother nursing a baby. The caption was, "Mother's milk is best for the child."

Imagine seeing a billboard like that in the United States?

"The thing that disgusts me," continues Corinne, "is that we don't have to take responsibility. We live so comfortably. And all these people saying, 'I'm not into politics'—really that's just sloth. I don't know—now I think I need another trip down there because I'm getting right back into all this. I mean, after Vietnam, didn't anybody learn? I thought we Americans GREW

UP. In Nicaragua, the feeling of being willing to die for something is intoxicating."

Bohrer shakes her head. "There was one thing people said to me over and over down there that showed the irony: 'Here's this little country that won this revolution for freedom, and yet the country that STANDS for freedom is trying to put them down.'"

~ 6 ~

Matagalpa

Yesterday I paid a visit to Ivania, the Mayor of Matagalpa's wife, who's a career counselor and mother of three tots.

Ivania, who Phoebe introduced me to last time, spent twenty-six years in LA, so her English is impeccable. She has a kind of formal informality and European grace. Kids scramble around her and a parrot hops from floor to backs of chairs, as her husband watches Saturday television and offers me a beer.

When talking about the revolution, Ivania has the same warrior-like concentration she had last time, revealing deep introspection about what can be done in relation to what must be done. We burrowed immediately into discussion of the war, something that in Nicaragua precludes (and includes) all personal business.

"Who are Nicaragua's most supportive allies?" I asked.

"Material support has been enormous from Sweden, Finland, Holland, Spain, East and West Germany, and Canada."

"Would any countries come to Nicaragua's aid under an American invasion?"

"Many Latin American countries would defend Nicaragua," she was certain. "Mexico, Venezuela, Peru, Chile, Panama, Brazil, even Guatemala."

"What about Cuba?" I asked.

"I don't think Cuba would help militarily because of the East-West complications that might be provoked."

"And what about all this talk about Cubans training and teaching here?" I probed.

"The Cubans have been extremely helpful," she answered. "Lots of Cubans initially came over to pitch in. But when the Americans were using the Cuban presence as a communist issue, all the teachers, two hundred of them, were sent back to Cuba by the Sandinistas—again, so as not to provoke East-West tensions."

"That was about a year and a half ago, wasn't it?" she asked her husband.

"Two," he answered.

Ivania rocked in her rocker. The children, content to just be home with Mom and Dad, made no demands. The youngest stumbled to the window to see if her *compañero* friend was out there, a Sandinista guard who watches a *commandante's* (government leader's) house across the street. He waved back.

"What's changed here in the last six months, in terms of the war?" I asked.

Part of Ivania's answer was clear to any returning visitor, but she was generous with details. "It's tightened economically," she said. "You can't get things you need." 30

> *30) On May 1, 1985, President Reagan announced that his administration perceived Nicaragua to be "an unusual and extraordinary threat to the national security and foreign policy of the United States," and declared a national emergency and a trade embargo against Nicaragua to "deal with that threat."*
>
> — *Wikipedia*

Ivania went on, "Before, even with shortages, you could still get stuff if you could afford to pay more in specialty stores. Now, for example, you can't get sanitary napkins at all. A woman can get a bag of ten every two months…. This is an impossible situation. The reason for this shortage is because those same materials, cotton and gauze, are used for hospitals, and hospitals must have priority. It's terrible though. Another thing we can't get is toilet paper. It is rationed, and a family like mine gets four rolls a month. This is like nothing. And I send one roll with Jose to school because there's none at his school."

This little country of 3.5 million people, half aged fourteen or less, has had to relearn its way of life. Formerly, Nicaragua enjoyed American commodities, placing no great value on aspirin, thermometers, infant formula, and other everyday items that have since vanished. "We were totally dependent on so many American products," Ivania continued, "things we don't produce in Nicaragua. True, some of them could only be afforded by the bourgeoisie, but many things, like deodorant, for example, were hard to do without when the embargo first began. Now, of course, we're making more things ourselves or importing them from Europe."

The Sandinista government had to start from scratch, continually developing new trade agreements wherever possible to satisfy specific needs. And one long-term advantage of these empty markets is that anything Nicaragua can learn to produce for herself, she will....

"But how does a country manage without deodorant?" I wondered aloud.

Ivania rolled her eyes, "It was a terrible problem. But we soon discovered that Milk of Magnesia works fabulously."

"Milk of Magnesia?"

"Yes, it's wonderful. You can use it as deodorant, you can put it on your skin to stop itching, and then if you happen to get indigestion, you can drink some, too."

"So the deodorant problem was solved?"

"No, we ran out of Milk of Magnesia."

"Other than shortages," Ivania went on, "the situation in general now is just more intense. We are prepared for the worst. We expect an American invasion and are preparing for the moment when things fall on us from the sky." She then explained how, in this event, eighteen local children, including her own, would be taken to an underground shelter at her sister's house nearby. Her sister would take care of the children while twenty other women would be responsible for helping invalids escape from hospitals and nursing homes; then, after that, finding and aiding the wounded. Each *barrio* (neighborhood) was organizing in similar fashion. "We are very organized," she said. "We have to be. All the men are already either soldiers or in the Reserve, so they would all be fighting. It would just be women and children at home."

"Wouldn't it be hard to separate yourself from your children at a time like that?" I asked, trying to fathom a mother rushing them to the shelter, then dashing back out into the street.

"No. For the adults there is no choice, everyone will be needed. And that's the safest place for the children. At least they'll be together."

A sinister cloud often passes over Nicaragua. The shadow of death comes close, like a wind. You look out over the low mountains and rooftops, listen to the children's feet clattering down the street, and...there's no way to guess which way it will all go.

After a silence, I asked Ivania, "Do you think there's hope for Nicaragua?"

"Oh yes," her face lifted. "That's the one thing Nicaragua has no shortage of."

Meanwhile, economically, almost everything hinges on the coffee crop. Right now, it's the one assured export, much of it grown in the area surrounding Matagalpa. Every able-bodied person is urged to help pick coffee beans during the winter harvest. And foreigners from the world over come to assist.

Yet, with the threat of Contra attacks, pickers in some regions are unsafe without rifles. Even with rifles. Therefore, the pickers who work in these zones receive military training and dress in army fatigues. For an unmentionable piece wage, these pickers burrow deep into coffee bushes, often at the edge of some remote field far in the hills. Rifles slung over their shoulders, for months they're bent over, lost from view, the better ones picking four bags a day.

Eighty kilometers from Matagalpa, out of one such group of armed pickers—lined up in a tiny tele-phone office to call home after six weeks in the fields—popped an American voice. Indistinguishable from his co-workers except for the blue eyes, Peter (from Minneapolis) told me of his "good luck" in being able to participate in an effort that, for national security pur-poses, is off-limits to foreigners, especially Americans. He'd wanted to help the revolution, he said, but had wished to be with the Nicaraguans and improve his Spanish rather than work with other foreigners. A Nic-araguan family he'd lived with in Managua had made it possible for him to join the armed pickers.

"But you never know," he said, "when you might look up into the face of a Contra. And you have only a split second to determine whether or not a stranger out there is a Contra. Having never seen one, how will you know? Maybe he's just some guy with a rifle. The minute he raises it, though, you're too late. So you've got that split second to shoot him, and if you don't, you might be dead."

Peter said all he can do is hope other pickers are with him if this happens, and that they'll somehow know whether or not to shoot.

The fighting goes on predominantly in the eastern half of the country. Matagalpa is the last town of any size west of the trouble. The landscape grows increasingly more dangerous as you move away from anywhere that protective soldiers are stationed in numbers.

Don, who only stays at Tom's house on infrequent runs to Matagalpa, works two and a half hours northeast. He's building an electric generator for a settlement named Cua. (Seven months later, Ben Linder would be killed in Cua.) [31 & 32]

31) Benjamin Linder was an American engineer developing public works in Nicaragua during the Sandinista People's Revolution when he was killed by Contras in 1987. In the 1980s, Nicaragua saw many American journalists and volunteer workers protesting the Reagan Administration's backing of the Contra guerrillas in their effort to overthrow the Sandinistas. Linder came to Nicaragua in 1983 after graduating college with a degree in engineering. He worked initially in Managua, then moved north and began building hydroelectric plants in El Cua, near the village of Jinotega and close to Honduras, where the Contras had headquarters. The Contras opposed this, but Linder built a turbine that led to great improvements.

— The New Yorker, September 23, 1996 *

* In 1996, was 'The New Yorker' intentionally missing the mark by still calling the Sandinista Government (elected eight years before Linder's death) a 'People's Revolution'?

32) Ben Linder (July 7, 1959 – April 28, 1987) was an American engineer. While working on a small hydroelectric dam in rural northern Nicaragua, he was killed by the Contras, a loose confederation of rebel groups funded by the U.S. government. Coming at a time when U.S. support for the Contras was already highly controversial, Linder's death made front page headlines around the world and further polarized opinion in the United States.

— Wikipedia

Today Don offered me a lift back down to Managua, where he has to pick up supplies. And having once ridden the bus, with several hundred other passengers, I jumped.

Leaving around ten, we set out in the open
Jeep. We had to circle the town to get out because a
children's parade was in gay procession commemorat-
ing the 125th anniversary of Central America's freedom from Spanish rule, a national holiday,

Don had affixed lengths of rope on either side
of the Jeep, from the windshield to the back, to hold
onto where doors might've been. And on those roads,
you do hold on. Despite grit particles blowing into
our eyes and mouths from the vehicle floor for the
duration, we felt fine in the way a Jeep and a good
companion guarantee. Surrendering instantly to the
bright blue day, neither of us was eager to get to Managua. Though somewhat leveled from the massive
1972 earthquake, and checkered with empty fields,
it's still a sprawling urban hub.

Winding off onto a dirt road, our first stop was
the village of Chaquitillo, outside of Sebaco. Here,
Don knew some of the children and picked up two
along the road. We then followed word of mouth
to his friend Eric's new house — "in Barrio Number
Five," according to one of the half-pints in back. The
child then informed us there were 4000 residents in
Chaquitillo, "Five *barrios* with 500 people each."

Don smiled, "We don't question these things."

Eric, a thin forty-three-year-old American,
priding himself in a life devoted to revolutions of
various orders, was pleased by our visit. Living as
the *Nicas* (Nicaraguans), he'd even scored one of
the new houses built for country folk. It consisted of

two rooms of cement and brick — one a kitchen with a
dirt floor and an open fire for cooking. Included was a
stone outhouse in back.

Eric had planted huge adjacent fields with every
type of vegetable, that had grown so abundantly that
impressed neighbors donated their own fields to his
agricultural acumen. Diversification of crops here is
a genuine key to a better future. And teaching that is
Eric's self-declared role in the revolution.

Neighborhood children seemed to use Eric's
living room as a thruway to his back yard where there
was an apple tree. And they'd depart, again through
the house, carrying handfuls. He had a house-guest,
too — a round, avuncular gent called Bart, who'd apparently accompanied him through several revolutions.

~ September 16, 1986

~ 7 ~

Random Volunteers

As I rocked in a hammock last night, back here at the Santos, the *Señora* strung one up beside me. I asked if she'd felt any war-related changes in the last six months. (Reading the papers every morning has revived my Spanish and I can again converse with locals.) She told me that in Managua the full Reserve Army—every man forty or under, with or without children—has been called for three months' training, in preparation for a *Yanqui* invasion. Her husband was one of the exempt few because he works independently, but most every other husband and father has had to go train in the hills outside of town, not to return home at all during the training. To visit the fathers, families may go out to the camps on Sundays. Meanwhile, at their job sites, these men are replaced by older guys, women, or young boys. And when the men do eventually return, their work places are in chaos since everything's been handled by someone who didn't know the job. Nobody likes it. "But there's no choice," the *Señora* said.

Today's paper corroborated this. "It's hard for the people to accept these conditions and impositions," the article said, "and the constant disintegration of everything familiar. But the fight is for freedom from imperialism."

Such is the battle cry. The Sandinista government attempts to bolster the population by continually focusing on strength and unity. And in some bizarre way, there is strength and unity, even if only in the Nicaraguan courage to stand up to the world's military giant. To the death.

Nicaraguan citizens don't have the leeway to just wait and see; they must prepare for a full-on invasion. Yet, simultaneously, any preparations being made by the U.S. for this same invasion likely wouldn't even be known about by American citizens.

~ *September 18, 1986, Managua*

The rainy season brings fat dark clouds that spill over daily. But unlike places like England, these showers are refreshing—without them, the heat is unbearable. Thick gushes of wind precede the rain, and of course lush greenness results, so there's little to dislike about the torrents. Even though the harsh sun regularly pierces through, the wet months seem preferable to the dry, barren winters.

Presently, I have a two-cot room to myself at the Santos, where the odd female roommate joins me for a night or two. The first was a woman who insisted on speaking only Spanish. Clearly no Nicaraguan, I asked if she was from Spain. "No, Holland," she replied in Spanish.

Coordinating a friendship program between a Dutch city and the city of Leon here, she's been in Nicaragua two years. Though the Dutch learn English in grade school, she adhered to a patient brand of Spanish with me, sticking to her own rulebook about gringo protocol. And I suppose it makes some degree of sense to speak the national tongue rather than English, particularly where English is the language of the enemy, so I bumbled along in mildly annoyed Spanish.

A few other gringos at the hostel were a Danish couple moving slowly north from Peru, and a New Zealand guy heading south from LA—all on those once-in-a-lifetime globe-trots people take in their twenties. Politically though, they were almost dangerously naive. While most foreigners here and all the *Nicas* (Nicaraguans) are glued to newspapers, televisions, and rifles, these folks are reading novels, smoking cigarettes, and wondering why everything's so down-trodden. Hard to comprehend how anyone would wander into a tumultuous hot-bed of a U.S.-sponsored war, oblivious to what's going on, and remain void of curiosity.

My next roomie was a studious young German named Petra. She communicated in an even mix of Spanish and English that she seemed to think was one or the other, but that I followed easily. Also through a friendship program—this one between a German university town and the south-central Nicaraguan village of Acoyapa—Petra had just completed six weeks on a brigade building a school. Down there, west of Lake

Nicaragua, she said they'd heard gunfire in the hills all the time; a constant battle was being fought. Six people from Acoyapa were killed during her stay. The towns-people were embittered by the killings, she said, and visited the graves trembling and shouting with anger. "It was a terrible thing to see these people. There was nothing we could do. And now the young boys of six-teen or seventeen have to go up into the hills. We were there long enough to get to know some of them. They didn't want to go, but they must because the war gets worse." She went on to say that most of the farmers out in the hills are not only isolated but unable to market their goods because the roads are too precarious to use at all.

After the well-publicized (in Nicaragua, but not even a sidebar anywhere else in the world) incident of three European *brigadistas* being killed last summer, the Contra stated they would no longer spare "interna-tionals." That's when Germany, France, Finland, and Switzerland announced they wouldn't continue offer-ing aid to Nicaragua if their volunteer citizens might be killed. Petra confirmed that the Sandinistas had, consequently, pulled all the foreigners, including Amer-icans, out of the rural areas, leaving the many building projects unfinished in the countryside. Anticipating how unhappy and flustered brigade worker-volunteers would be to have to leave, the Sandinistas went to each project site and simply instructed everyone to come im-mediately with them to the nearest big town. (In a war, you do what soldiers tell you, you don't ask questions.)

So the *brigadistas* went with them to the cities, but were then prohibited from going back to their rural projects. Their belongings were retrieved for them by the soldiers.

According to Petra, numerous brigade workers are now in search of other projects to participate in, in the cities, where *internationalistas* are still permitted. Her group, because they were already in a city, was the only one in that region allowed to continue working. But now her job was completed, and she would spend a month exploring a bit. Then she'd go back to Germany and, through her university, start another friendship program with another Nicaraguan village.

She said the solidarity movement in West Germany is vast, despite the German government's pro-Reagan position. And Daniel Ortega, or "Daniel" as he's known, is at this moment in East Germany reaffirming the solid alliance with that nation.

After two nights, Petra headed off for the Atlantic coast. I didn't envy her that ordeal. There's no through-road to the east coast, except for a dirt one up north that goes through the *zona de guerra* (war zone), currently off-limits to all but military. So there's just one paved road that only goes as far as a village called Rama, six hours east of Managua. From Rama, travelers to the East Coast must transfer to a riverboat for a five-hour voyage to Bluefields, a small town on the Caribbean coast. Trouble is, in order to transport passengers all the way from Managua to Bluefields in one day, the single daily bus from Managua must depart at 4:20 a.m.

If that doesn't promise fatigue, to get a seat on said bus for your half-day ride to Rama, you have to buy tickets the morning before. The ticket office opens at 6 a.m., but you have to be on line at 5 to guarantee a seat. For anyone still feeling chipper about this day-trip, the bus station is a half hour taxi ride from the Santos, and finding a cab at 4:30 a.m. is the final test of your determination. So, instead, it's advised to sleep on the concrete pavement at the bus station the night before (with droves of others)…even though the next night, of course, you'll sleep there again, to queue up at 3:30 a.m. for your hard-won seat on the bus.

This is the sole method for getting to the east coast. That is, after applying for permission, i.e., xeroxing your passport, paying a fee, filling out a form, then waiting five or more working days for approval.

Unfortunately for Petra and her friend, they had to set out in pelting rain, so snagging a dry spot for their sleeping bags would be yet another occasion to re-avow their zeal. Or back out.

~ *September 21, 1986, Managua*

Part Four –
The Coast, the Ghost, and the Boat

~ 8 ~

San Juan del Sur

I overheard two gringo guys chatting in the lobby of the Intercontinental. The one talking had the certainty, the facts, the khakis, and the ironed shirt of academic credibility. I caught snippets like "socialism," "the people," and "here in Nicaragua." The listener was the New Zealand tourist from the Santos, getting a crash course in 'The Fundamentals of Human Rights'—daily discourse in Nicaragua, flowing more freely than drinking water. But the unsuspecting tourist had clearly taken interest. "Dear Mom, I went for the guacamole and I stayed for the Revolution."

Eric and Bart (the roving revolutionaries from Chaquitillo) and I had cooked up a plan to share a cab from Managua down to San Juan del Sur, a village on the southwest coast. The following Friday, we set out.

Since the fare was only 40,000 *cordobas* for the three-hour drive (not wildly inexpensive for Nicaragua, but only about $20), and since this country is "The Land of Lakes and Volcanos," and volcanic energy defines the place, we paid a visit to the smoke-issuing summit of one active volcano just south of Managua, then passed an inactive one south of the city of Massaya.

From there, we continued west to the untainted and unpainted beach town of San Juan del Sur, where 10,000 buckets of color and twenty well-placed trash-cans would make it Shangri-La.

But, in Nicaragua, every place needs an overhaul, because there's no paint, no money, no men to do the work, and no American imports (not even hammers and nails). So the country's in shambles. In San Juan del Sur, roads are disintegrating and all the unpainted wood deteriorating. But the town curves around a wide, still bay, and its small, easy-going population and happy kids scampering on the long beach make it peaceful despite the war. And such a pretty place not catering to tourism is so rare.

In relation to the war, the prevailing view is that this remote southwestern corner of the country is safe. Yet the town's isolation and it being the second largest port in Nicaragua made it seem, to me at least, a like-ly target by sea, or even by aerial assault.... But Eric affirmed it's well guarded, pointing out military lookout posts with anti-aircraft weaponry on both endpoints of the bay, Coast Guard patrol boats, and soldiers sta-tioned all around town. He said there's also a military base around the cape on the next beach. And, to supple-ment the defense, Bart and I were stormed in the street last night by ten bare-footed soldiers carrying flags and crying, "*Viva la Revolution!*" A squad of little boys would repeatedly thunder past us from the rear, then stop up ahead, taking formation in neat rows. As we'd pass, they'd suggest a photo. We'd have happily obliged but it was pitch dark. When I explained that we needed light, the shirtless troops with their Sandinista flags and shiny eyes proposed using the headlights of a passing Army Jeep. But alas, we had no cameras either.

Earlier, we'd supped in an outdoor tavern where, below the table, a cat, a dog, a toad, and her young one were situated, along with swarms of mosquitoes. Eric, storehouse of Nicaraguan history, who's lived in various parts of the country for two years, including five months here in San Juan del Sur, told of a particular Contra battle in the summer of 1985 up near Chaquitillo. He'd gotten the story from a Sandinista soldier friend who'd been sent out directly afterwards to collect the bodies.

Every bridge in Nicaragua, no matter its size, Eric explained, is guarded by two to twelve Sandinista soldiers. In that instance, a small regimen of Contras, supported by a larger platoon nearby, ambushed the bridge outside Sebaco, killing all the guards. Then, stashing their weapons, these same few Contras made their way to a remote village called Trinidad, not far off, where they strolled into a cafe for a beer. As they sat around a table nonchalantly swilling their brew, the cafe owners and a couple of neighbors quickly and discreetly assessed that since no one recognized them nor knew anything about them, and they obviously weren't tourists or travelers, nor did they appear to have business

in Trinidad, they must be Contras. The townspeople
decided to play dumb until the men left town, in hopes
of avoiding trouble. They let the Contras eat and drink
undisturbed, but meanwhile sent messengers to alert
the local Army.

Once fortified, the Contras ambled out of the
village. The Sandinista soldiers who'd been summoned
trailed at a distance, all the way up through the hills to
where the Contras were camped. Sandinistas from outlying areas had also been radioed in. Noiselessly, they
all surrounded the camp, then closed in for an attack. A
battle ensued and the Sandinistas won. Afterwards, Eric's friend was sent out to the battlefield where he found
only three or four dead Sandinistas amidst some 300
bodies of Contras. Among those 300, were the bodies of
three gringos.

Contras don't wear any ID, so those gringos
could've been anybody—foreign mercenaries, American
"advisors," CIA agents. One thing was certain, though,
they weren't Central Americans....

The has-been Hotel Estrella, one of few hotels
in town, is a white and blue waterfront establishment.
With half-arch windows, aqua trim, and balconies
above the beach and palms, it's lovely in a neglected
way—traces of grandeur, lost elegance, art gone to seed.
In fact, many of the run-down Nicaraguan buildings
exude former style.

The Estrella houses maybe five other gringos,
mostly European, aside from skinny Eric, enormous
Bart, and myself—curious trio, eliciting hushed com-

mentary when we file through the lobby, particularly as we're sharing one room.

But, were there a soundtrack at the Estrella, aside from the sounds of waves, wind, and children playing, the music would be low notes in a minor key—maybe a harpsichord, a quiet oboe, and organ chords. The huge blue rooms, scrubbed blond wooden tables, extra high ceilings with criss-cross beams, are all grayed slightly by a ghost contingent that has nocturnal run of the place. This became clear to me last night after an eerie foray down the unlit passageway to the restroom.

After about age five, it's infrequent that you're frightened to come out of the bathroom at night, but I was frozen in there, weak in the knees about re-entering that hallway. Subsequent visits were even less fun. And by morning I said to Eric, "This joint's positively jumpin' with entities."

He smiled knowingly and told me that years ago, an enterprising Nicaraguan couple purchased the hotel as a business. The man soon hired a young local woman as a chambermaid and, needless to say, began an affair with her. The wife found out and left him. He then married the chambermaid and they had kids together. Considerably older than she, in time he died and left her the hotel. But, after his death, the first wife returned, wanting her share of the property. Embittered by the past (and entitled to a portion of the property), she posed a problem for the second wife. Such a problem, that one of the second wife's sons grabbed a rifle one day and put an end to the matter.

The second wife, elderly now, is still the proprietress. And though her son remains in jail for murder, his wife and child also reside at The Estrella. So, one or two of the spooks floating around were identified. But even by day, a dankness lingers in what might otherwise be a splendid seaside accommodation.

Today's one of those select few you have to wander far to find. An almost forgotten tranquility inhabits this palmy cove—placid waters of clear green-gray-blue, pelicans skimming crests of modest waves, then diving like arrows for fish. There are almost no cars—only military vehicles filing through, ironically more welcome than upsetting. (And a few more wouldn't hurt.) But, generally, everyone walks, cycles, or rides horses, and even the passing soldiers are relaxed.

Children scatter, scurry, and scramble underfoot—it's practically a children's town. But they don't fight or cry or even seem to have parents. Unattached four-year-old boys bound through outdoor cafes, then across the beach and back, oblivious to adults. Clusters of unattended baby girls sit in circles digging holes along the tideline. I'm aware that half of Nicaragua's 3.5 million people are age fourteen or less, but in San Juan del Sur it seems three quarters of the residents are under age nine.

~ September 21, 1986, San Jorge

The gap between what needs to be done in Nicaragua and what's being done is shocking. If it wasn't for the message of hope coming through the media, this government probably would no longer exist.

As a foreigner, observing this standard of life is depressing, but being a Nicaraguan must be close to impossible. Those in possession of anything at all—if there is such a group—are a rare and separate breed. In Managua, everyone's accustomed to gringos, but outside of the capital you have to take off your jewelry and even your watch. Not because they steal, but because you're flaunting the difference between yourself and them…. Everything about you—your flip-flops, your water bottle, your backpack, your relatively new shirt, even your pen—are what everybody needs. A camera is a symbol of wealth. Yet, compared to people in the countryside, even Managuans seem all dressed up, just by owning shoes and clothes without holes.

When you consider what it will take to lift this place up, and that first the U.S. government has to be abated somehow, it's difficult to retain hope.

And this lends confusion to one's role here as a gringo….

Indeed, Nicaragua is enhanced by the international atmosphere, foreigners a welcome and complimentary aspect of the revolution. The presence of the myriad journalists and volunteers is invited and cherished; gringo contributions, from schools to houses to clinics to bicycles, are hugely appreciated, desperately needed, and made use of far and wide. Yet, for individual Nicaraguans, who you'd love to personally help somehow, their needs are so all-encompassing you can't possibly make a difference. And it's painful drawing the line about what you can and can't affect.

I suppose it's an option to give all you have and slip into the have-not position yourself, but to what avail? Probably best to do your work and meet the Nicaraguans halfway, reminding yourself what you're here for. And then, should you decide to stay, rework your life priorities and figure out how to get by amongst such poor people while still doing your job and keeping a mental balance. But it's easy to get heartsick witnessing such quantities of nothing—kids playing with nothing, people wearing rags, cars breaking down never to run again, and men drinking too much beer because beer exists.

It's not at all fair to live amongst these people while being exempt from the suffering. That you can and will 'go home' is the unspoken truth. But they don't begrudge you that. Still, it remains…and you'll never really get into their skin. That's the quiet guilt foreigners live with here. But it drives you to do what little you can.

The government tries hard to help the people. But all resources go to the war, from Jeeps to military uniforms to arms. It's a horrible trade-off.

And, later on, what does a country do *after* establishing such a mega militia as Nicaragua has had to? Not that easy to rotate back to ordinary civilian daily living; reality itself has so radically shifted.

~ late September, 1986, San Juan del Sur

~ 9 ~

CIA

There's a paranoid gringo pastime down here that I call "the CIA game." We invented it on the Peace March during our hold-over in Managua, based on the fact that since there *are* agents down here, *somebody* has to be one! [33] So from time to time — in jest, but y'never know — some gringo will question the credibility of some other gringo.

33) *Reports of secret operations along the Nicaragua-Honduras border have circulated for months. But 'Newsweek' has uncovered extensive details of a campaign that has escalated far beyond Washington's original intentions. Administration sources reveal that there are now almost 50 CIA personnel serving in Honduras. That team is supplemented by dozens of operatives including a number of retired military and intelligence officers. The forces are drawn from...an estimated 10,000 anti-Sandinistas in Nicaragua itself and supporters of deposed dictator Anastasio Somoza. Their forays are designed*

*to harass the Sandinistas while CIA operatives
cast around for a moderate new Nicaraguan
leadership.*

— Newsweek, November 8, 1982

Yesterday, as I sat writing in a seaside cafe, a new
Norteamericano walked in alone and sat down with a
Pepsi. About forty, with good posture, khaki shirt with
epaulets, and new sneakers, he had CIA all over him.
He drank his soda just like army personnel—eight good
swigs—and seemed to have nothing to do but scan the
harbor, scrutinizing the end point where a Coastguard
boat and soldiers are deployed. He even donned pre-
scription sunglasses for a sharper (or more discreet)
view.

Any other gringo, some *brigadista* from Europe
or North America, would be writing letters, talking
to locals or each other, or just having a bite. This guy,
clean and efficient, with crew cut, trimmed mustache,
and a good tan, had no small business whatsoever—no
bathing suit, no camera, no grubby backpack.

Downing the Pepsi, he continued studying the
panorama, then got up, paid, uttered a well-pronounced
'*gracias*,' and split. I watched as he crossed the prom-
enade then entered the hostel directly across from our
place. Later, as I swam around the bay, I decided to
keep an eye on this cat.

Returning to the Estrella after my swim, I spotted him on the second floor of his hostel. He'd strate-
gically arranged a corner room, from which to observe
the complete bay, and was taking in the whole scene

from his balcony hammock. Only his feet were visible from below, but he obviously missed nothing through the hammock netting.

I relayed this to Bart and Eric, who had a chuckle and then, at my coaxing, took turns ambling to our lobby door to discreetly check the guy out.

"All I could see was a pair of feet," Bart reported back.

"We should track his movements," I said, rounding up players for my game. "Between the three of us, we could collect conclusive info. But since he's watching everything, we should only enter and leave our hotel one at a time, so he doesn't know we're together."

Bart then volunteered to ask the guy later to pose for a picture. He'd say he needed a shot of a typical American tourist to prove to his wife that Nicaragua isn't so dangerous.

Great!

That afternoon, we three chose a nearby eatery for lunch. Awaiting our grub, and feeling generally alright, a voice behind me suddenly said, "Are you guys following me around?"

I turned squarely into the face of the CIA agent! Close up, he looked even more undercover—sturdy, serious, and surely packing a pistol. Feigning deafness, I whirled the other way.

The man then pulled out a chair at the next table. As I squirmed and cleared my throat trying to get Bart's and Eric's attention, they made the mistake of politely acknowledging the guy—unaware who he was, having only seen his feet. I nudged Bart's sandal under the table. "That's HIM!" I hissed.

Bart smiled right past me at the spy, and all I could do was hope he'd do some fast talking.

"Didn't we pass you hitching on the road up by Sebaco?" Bart then asked him. (Good one.)

"Hitch-hiking, right, perfect cover," I thought.

"Yeah," Eric chimed in, "you're the guy who won't ride the buses. Have a seat."

To my utmost discomfort, Eric now offered the agent a seat at *our* table. I conjured up a phony name for when they introduced me.

"Only in Nicaragua I won't ride the buses," said the spy. "I ride 'em in Honduras, Guatemala, Mexico, anywhere else. Too crowded here."

"Intimate with all the war zones," I thought.

The guy then embarked on a lengthy and descriptive account of a recent canoe trip he'd taken, solo for 411 days, from Oregon to New York, via Miami. He went on to discuss his dissatisfaction with, and eventual departure from, the Weyerhaeuser Corporation, a huge U.S. timber company based in Washington State, from which he'd been let go with $17,000 severance pay. The cat's name was Dean and, traveling alone by buses and hitching, he was now heading overland to Patagonia. He was, it turned out, just another adventurer passing through.

Though amusing, the CIA game rarely (like never) produces a bona fide agent. Then again, if they were easy to identify, they wouldn't be doing their job.

~ *September 22, 1986, San Juan del Sur*

Little did I know the obvious place where CIA are embedded: right in plain sight. The following piece is based on a book, written years later. But the moment I saw it, I knew where the CIA had been in Nicaragua. [34]

34) from: "Confession from the Profession:
  'Presstitutes' in the service of the CIA,"
  by Tim Pelzer, 11-19-2020:

It is well documented that the CIA uses the media to spread disinformation. After 1945, in what is known as "Operation Mockingbird," the agency recruited journalists in major US media to promote its Cold War anti-communist perspective. According to former CIA agent turned whistle-blower Philip Agee, the agency had journalists on its payroll across Latin America. In the book, "Presstitutes: Embedded in the Pay of the CIA," (published in 2013), Udo Ulfkotte, a former editor for a German daily newspaper (Frankfurter Algemeine Zeitung or FAZ), reveals how the CIA and the German Intelligence Agency (BND) use the German media to spread propaganda to shape public opinion.

The BND recruited Ulfkotte while he was in university, then placed him at the newspaper. As a naive young man, he was thrilled to work for his country's intelligence agency. "However, looking back," said Ulfkotte, "I was corrupt, I was manipulative and dealt in disinformation."

The CIA and BND (the "extended arm" or "subsidiary' of the CIA, according to Ulfkotte) told him what stories to write, supplying him with information he never verified, all under the full knowledge of those papers' editors and owners.

On one occasion in 2005, then CIA Director James Woolsey told Ulfkotte to write articles saying that the US did not carry out industrial espionage (to cover up US spying on German companies). Ulfkotte said, "The FAZ (newspaper) expressly encouraged me to strengthen my contact with the western intelligence services and was delighted when I signed my name to the pre-formulated reports that I sometimes received from them." Another fake story Ulfkotte placed his name on was about Libyan leader Moammar Gaddafi building a poisonous gas factory with the help of European companies in 1993.

"Yes," he confessed, "looking back, I was exploited and became one of the perpetrators who was fed materials from the outside. I was influencing public opinion through the mass media —I just didn't want to believe it back then."

Ulfkotte claims that his fellow German journalists, both in Germany and abroad, continue spreading disinformation through the CIA and BND. But if they want to remain employed, it's impossible for anyone in the German media to evade the clutches of the spy agencies. Journalists who refuse to work for the BND can legally be fired.

While working in the Middle East as a foreign correspondent, Ulfkotte discovered that "every foreign reporter for the American and British press was also active for their intelligence services."

He said intelligence services believe journalists are easy to buy, and one CIA agent told the Washington Post, "You can get a journalist for less than a good whore, for a few hundred dollars."

U.S. intelligence since the 1950s also established a wide range of charitable foundations in Germany. "All of them have one primary goal: establishing intelligence agency outposts under the guise of philanthropic institutions. Here, agents are perceived as employees of these foundations; their purpose, to exert pro-American influence on future German elites and, wherever possible, make them susceptible to blackmail."

According to Ulfkotte, "The war in Iraq, the Guantanamo Bay reality, and drone executions are absolutely incompatible with German law." But German journalists working through pro-U.S. organizations "become partial advocates and/or lobbyists for a foreign value system" which accounts for German media support for participation in foreign wars alongside the U.S. Ulfkotte stated, "These journalists manufacture pro-U.S. opinion pushing for war with Russia."

Ulfkotte regretted his participation in the German media, which he called "the propaganda arm of U.S. imperialism." He said, "I'm ashamed of having worked for these war-mongers for a good portion of my journalistic life."

Like all whistleblowers, Ulfkotte paid a heavy price for publishing his book. Not only was he fired from his job at FAZ and banished from working in the media, but he said the German police conducted frequent searches of his house. In 2017, he died from a "heart attack" at age 56.

"Presstitutes" was a bestseller in Germany for 18 months when it was first published in 2013, despite being ignored by mainstream media.

~ 10 ~

Smart Gringos

At 7 a.m. on Sunday, Bart, Eric, and I, insepa-
rable unit that we'd become, hopped in the back of a
tarpaulin-covered truck (standard rural bus) with forty
other passengers (including two newborns), twenty of
whom were standing. We'd decided to visit the volca-
nic island of Ometepe in the middle of enormous Lake
Nicaragua (easy to spot on the map), and headed out
in the rain down a dirt road to the village of Rivas.
One intimate hour later, we arrived at the Rivas market, competed for a taxi, and finally got one to the lake
shore four kilometers off. There we lunched, stayed dry
during a second rain, waited two and a half hours, then
boarded the ferry.

The boats and gangplanks were the shabbiest
I've ever seen, though I've not been to India. Again
I was glad not to have to apologize for Nicaragua to
some cringing companion I'd lured down here. At
times things seem 'backwards' to an almost unneces-
sary degree—this narrow wobbly wooden plank, over
which heavily laden mothers and terrified tots had to
cross—a graphic example. The smallest attention to
the issue could've yielded a safer way of getting people

onto the boat. On the other hand, the fact that things aren't made easier (ever) is fine for most of us. Even Bart, with a leg injury, recent stomach cancer operation, and his huge belly (that leaves a wake of giggling children wherever we go) finds it all quite okay. Minor risks and inconveniences are truly negligible; Nicaraguan people have graver concerns.

The boat was crowded, the lake choppy, the air balmy and hot. It was good to be on the water. Lake Nicaragua is gigantic and Ometepe a sizable isle in the middle of it. On the horizon ahead, the two great volcanoes on Ometepe hung from the clouds down to the lake. There was something tame about sailing on clear water to an island inside the same country, and tameness is a relief around here. The Contra haven't attacked Ometepe yet and, as Eric says, they'd have little motivation to. Should they somehow manage to capture the island, they'd be converged upon from all sides.

We disembarked after an hour afloat and took rooms in the portside hostel for 800 *cordobas* each (about 35 cents). We then meandered around the village of Moyogalpa and when a bus came along, hopped on to quickly view the island before sundown.

"Where are you going?" asked the driver.

"Where's the next stop?"

"San Marco."

"Okay, three tickets to San Marco," we chirped, taking seats on the small, half-empty bus. It was already clear that few gringos found their way to this dot on the map. Now, as we bumped along the dirt road, passing thatched huts on either side, our fellow passengers tried unsuccessfully to hide their fascination with us, particularly spherical Bart.

The shyness in the eyes and smiles of the islanders, their childlike curiosity, embraced us. With black Indian hair and smooth skin stretched over noses and cheeks, their faces had unspoiled loveliness. Meanwhile, we were entranced by their world of grass huts, lush vegetation, horse-drawn carts, and big black lava stones mixed into the earth.

The bus halted wherever someone wanted to get off, and eventually there was no one left but us, the driver, and the young ticket-taker. Just as I was wondering how mighty a metropolis San Marco could be with not one local going there, the bus pulled into a cul-de-sac encircled by three huts, and stopped. There was little sign of life and we gringos just sat in the empty bus gazing out into the palm jungle.

"San Marco," announced the conductor.

We looked at each other, sucking in our cheeks to keep straight faces. Now we knew why everyone had regarded us with such wonder.... We were going to San Marco? Whatever for?

"Where is the bus going next?" I asked the driver, who politely pretended visitors to San Marco were a dime a dozen.

"Altagracia," he replied.

We shrugged at each other.

"Is Altagracia a bigger town than San Marco?" I asked the driver.

"*Sí*," he said and laughed. So off we went.

"The Three Stupidos," said Bart, "that's what we're going to call ourselves."

As we circled the island en route to the other side, a low cloud hovered around the nearby volcano, a cloud that changed configurations dramatically but never lifted.

As we de-bussed in Altagracia, the child ticket-taker told Eric the bus would be back at 5:00. It was now 4:00, so we'd have just enough time to see the village and still get back to our hotel by nightfall. But after a muddy walk to the shore and a saunter around the sparse town, the bus didn't return. In a row, we waited on a roadside bench, but by 5:25 still no bus. Nor any other vehicles. Asking a few villagers what time the bus would return, we learned that, indeed, it would be back at 5—5 in the morning.

"The Three Stupidos," said Bart with disgust, as we resumed our positions on the bench. We were a forty-five-minute drive from our Moyogalpa hotel, the sun was setting, and there were no accommodations here in Altagracia.

Leaving the other Stupidos on the bench, I ran up and down the quiet street in my fuchsia rain poncho in search of a ride back. I found two parked trucks, but both drivers said they weren't going anywhere. Seeing a white Jeep parked about five blocks up, I ran toward it and asked around for its owner. A bartender said it belonged to a man named Chico who was in the house across the street. He suggested I knock on the door. That seemed a bit intrusive, so I just lingered outside hoping Chico might come out.

In moments the door opened and two men stepped into the street. "Chico?" I timidly approached them.

"No," said one. He had a nice smile though, and because we were desperate I told him in faulty Spanish the plight of The Three Stupidos. His smile widened. And by the time I got to asking for a lift, because he was in fact the Jeep driver, he said, "Of course."

I raced back to collect my fat and thin friends and we trundled back up the street and clambered into the Jeep, that by now contained two other people in addition to the first two. The sight of Bart raised eyebrows all around—maybe I should have warned them that we three were the equivalent of four or five. But after looking at each other with twisted smiles, and muttering things like, *"mucho comida"* (much food), they packed us in.

The nice driver, Orlando, chatted with us as we continued around the volcano in the dark, taking the long way back to Moyogalpa, dropping off riders hither and yon. I commented that I hadn't seen many soldiers on Ometepe Island, and asked Orlando if he considered the island safe from Contra attacks. He replied that the island was very *calma* and always had been. "But we're prepared to fight," he said. "Everyone on the island is in the militia, and whoever doesn't have a gun will use stones. And we have *a lot* of stones."

It turned out the charming Orlando was the island's head of the FSLN (the Sandinista Army).

Sensing we'd probably enjoyed the lion's share of Ometepe's tourist attractions—riding the bus to San Marco, basically—plus met the head of the FSLN—we decided to head back on a watermelon boat the next afternoon.

About forty minutes into the crossing, halfway across Lake Nicaragua, the water pump broke. Now the engine would neither run nor pump water out. There was no translator aboard, only the eight crew members and three other passengers, but we and the watermelons were clearly sitting heavily on the lake, more of it flooding over the sides as we heaved to and fro.

Two men scrambled down to the engine compartment below and occasionally shouted up to the captain, who'd then re-try the motor, to no avail.

Exactly halfway between the island and the mainland, we were three to five miles from land.

After a good while, Bart noted my furrowed brow and pointed out that the watermelons would be sacrificed before the boat would be allowed to sink, and so far no one was pitching them overboard. As big swells gushed over the sides though, it seemed we might flip onto one side, or simply be submerged. Massive black storm clouds stacked overhead and there wasn't another vessel in sight. My only comfort was that these men knew more than I about things maritime (even Bart was a lifelong seaman), and were all staying *calma*. Eric told me that there were life jackets (somewhere), but I still feared the loss of my camera, journal, and typewriter should we have to start dog-paddling.

With the green melons nestled in rows in the red boat interior, bobbing on the gray water with a perfect pointed volcano in the background and dark clouds above, the scene was at least photogenic. In the boat were all the muscular sailors, mocha without shirts, black eyes set in square serious faces. And smack in the middle sat Bart, a blue-eyed Santa in his short shorts, Hawaiian shirt, orange bandana, and cowboy hat.

After an hour of laboring with the engine, the sailors got it going. And off we sailed, relieved smiles all around.

~ *September 24, 1986, San Juan del Sur*

Part Five – More Back Story

~ 11 ~

Commies

Soviet Influence [35]

35) Writing articles for Life Magazine in June 1946, Foster Dulles began painting an increasingly more frightening picture of the Soviet threat. In "Thoughts on Soviet Conduct and What to Do about It," he claimed, "Soviet leaders have launched a worldwide campaign aimed to subjugate the West, to eliminate the essentials of free society, and to impose a system repugnant to our ideals of humanity and fair play." The Soviets, he maintained, had a shadowy network of allies in non-communist countries who pretended to be patriots but took guidance from Moscow.

Dulles' urgent tone amped up the intensity of how most Americans would view the world for a generation. And Soviet communism became the unseen force directing nationalist U.S. movements in Asia, Africa, and Latin America.

*— from: "The Brothers—John Foster Dulles,
Allen Dulles, and Their Secret World War,"
by Stephen Kinzer*

The more one researches the grandiloquence of power moguls like the Dulles brothers, the more one perceives communist scare tactics as, plain and simple, a smokescreen for flat-out imperialism, as well as a political headliner to gain Congressional support and funding.

Since it's universally *uncool* to casually topple foreign governments to appropriate their resources—even if you're the United States of America—you need a 'reason' why you're doing it. You need 'bad guys' to fight off. You need 'politics' to illustrate how you're going in there to save the poor souls suffering under those VERY BAD people (thousands of miles from our homeland, but we're next).

That's where 'fear' works its magic—you come up with something scary enough to convince first Congress, then the citizenry, that we must slap this little tropical country upside the head or else the whole world will soon be conquered by Commies. (And, besides, who doesn't like bananas?)

To this day, 'communism' works brilliantly at freaking everybody out. "Seems like every time America needs a distraction, it's always Russia, Russia, Russia. Here we go again." [36]

*36) Said by a trucker in the U.S. Truckers
Convoy to D.C., Feb. 28, 2022, as the U.S.
media took on the war in the Ukraine.*

In that same vein,

37) ...*In 1947, siting Soviet pressure on Greece and Turkey, President Truman decided the U.S. should make a new commitment to intervene anywhere in the world to stop "the spread of communism."*

"Mr. President," prompted a Senator named Vandenburg, "the only way you're ever going to get this is to make a speech and scare the hell out of the country."

Truman then unveiled to Congress what became the Truman Doctrine: "Totalitarian regimes imposed on free peoples, by direct or indirect aggression, undermine the foundations of international peace and, hence, the security of the United States. ...It must be the policy of the United States to support free peoples."

Accordingly, Congress then awarded Truman his $400,000,000 request for military aid to countries where communist influence was seen to be growing.

Some historians pinpoint this as the moment when the United States proclaimed the entire world a battleground between the super powers, and the Cold War began in earnest.

...Never in history have a few men in a single country achieved such worldwide influence.

— from: "The Brothers—John Foster Dulles, Allen Dulles, and Their Secret World War," by Stephen Kinzer

And jumping ahead forty years—to the Contra War:

> *38) Elliott Abrams (Assistant Secretary of State under President Reagan) believed communist governments were the worst human rights violators in the world. ...This theory allowed the Reagan administration to rationalize supporting murderous regimes so long as they were anti-Communists.*
>
> — *American University political scientist, William M. LeoGrande*

'Communism' became America's global culprit, blamed for social unrest, political upheaval, and common people rebelling against tyrannical rule. "The Commies caused this turmoil. WE didn't cause the discontent. WE didn't sponsor dictators. WE didn't murder anyone with opposing views—it's another communist takeover. But don't worry, WE'RE going to save everybody. (We just need you American patriots to pay the billions for the military. Just the small price of freedom.)"

Even according to the CIA's own website: [39]

> *39) Assessing the role of Communists in a revolutionary situation takes special care, because their noise and dramatic presence may not be based on much actual strength and popular appeal.*

—"The Bogotazo," by Jack Davis, July 2, 1996,
CIA Historical Review Program ('CIA.gov')

But, probably more significantly, the Soviet Union—without whom WWII would likely have been lost by our side, and to whom we all owe a gargantuan debt of gratitude—was, for many years after that hideous war, doggedly rebuilding their nation. In World War II, the Soviet Union not only endured horrendous battles on their land, but suffered some 27 MILLION casualties, far more than any other country, not to mention 14 MILLION wounded soldiers, and total decimation of their cities and country. Yet this tragedy was largely ignored at the time by that Washington faction busily brokering pirate-style deals in third world countries via 'communist' scare tactics.

A nation in triage, Russia was hardly out conquering the world in those years. It was licking its horrific wounds, trying to recover from unimaginable loss, mind-bending death tolls, and earth-shattering destruction…for a long, long time.

The Bogotazo

Few today are familiar with 'the bogotazo'—an event that began with an assassination and became a Western Hemisphere influencer.

'Seemingly' not orchestrated by the USA, nor apparently a coup, it was a political incident in Bogota, Colombia characterized mainly by interminable unrest.

(A coup is a sudden, forceful, unexpected replacement of a government with a new government — such as the one the U.S. pulled off in Guatemala in 1954.)

To summarize: In the spring of 1948, Colombia was experiencing classic pre-election politics of conservatives versus liberals, with the usual array of alternative parties, fringe ideologies, and the full scope of egos, ideals, personalities, and hot debate. (Calls for the overthrow of 'Yankee Imperialism' were part of the soundtrack.)

The favored liberal candidate, expected to win, was a practicing attorney with the last name of Gaitan. On April 9, 1948, outside his law office, he was shot and killed by a lone gunman.

A ten-hour riot followed the shooting, destroying much of downtown Bogota and other nearby towns, killing somewhere between 600-3000 people and hospitalizing hundreds more. 157 downtown buildings were damaged, 103 destroyed completely.

And, unbelievably, from the moment of the assassination, and for *years* to follow, aggression and factionalism continued. Because, after the loss of such a favored leader, and then all the rioting and mayhem, Colombia couldn't find its balance. Alcoholism and poverty remained rampant, the majority directionless, and rebellious floundering scarred the entire era. The bogotazo was a dark stain on Colombian history, revealing the country's extreme political unrest, bitterness, and animosity.

To this day, facts about the assassination remain unconfirmed. But the timing was suspect because that same week in Bogota, the 9th annual Pan-American Conference was underway, with twenty-one countries from the Americas in attendance. [40]

> *40) The bogotazo outbreak was clearly the spontaneous reaction of partisan citizens already on edge as a result of acute political tensions and party violence. The disturbances which interrupted the Pan-American Conference are more properly attributable to the basic political and economic tensions prevalent in Latin America than to international Communist conspiracy.*
>
> — *from: "Review of the World Situation as it Relates to the Security of the United States" (May 12, 1948)*

On the CIA's website,[41] too, it's acknowledged that neither the real reason for the assassination nor the actual perpetrator(s) were ever determined.

> *41) The Communists were neither strong enough nor popular enough to take command of Colombia.*
>
> *...Throughout nearly all its history, power in Colombia has been monopolized by a small elite. But in 1948 it was closer to social revolution than ever before or since. The Colombian government, though, blamed the bogotazo riots on Communist agitation and foreign intrigue, rather than addressing the underlying causes of popular discontent.*

*Twenty years later, however, the same elite
still controlled Colombia.*

— *"The Bogotazo," by Jack Davis, July 2, 1996,
CIA Historical Review Program (CIA.gov)*

*42) It has been theorized that the as-
sassination was planned for political reasons,
but this has never been corroborated. Numerous fingers have also been pointed at Colombia's then President Ospina who was challeng-
ing Gaitan in the upcoming election; other sec-
tors of Gaitan's same political party; the Colombia Communist party; Fidel Castro (who'd
held a meeting in Bogota with his supporters
that same morning); and* [wait for it]...*the CIA.*

– *Wikipedia*

But the incident was relevant to Nicaragua because it occasioned the U.S. to sound off about "communism penetrating the Western Hemisphere," or Commies breaching our shores. (Despite the USSR being a
nation in tatters.)

For the Dulles brothers, Ike, Nixon, United Fruit,
and Sullivan and Cromwell, the bogotazo was practically a gift from God. According to Secretary of State Mar-
shall, who attended the Pan-American Conference:

*43) What happened in Bogota was not
merely a Colombian or Latin American incident*

*but a world affair, and a lurid illustration of the
length to which Russia is willing to go in its (no
longer cold) war against the democracies.*

— *New York Times editorial, April 14, 1948*

The way the bogotazo was used politically by the
U.S. helps explain *all* the on-going conflicts between
the U.S. and its southern neighbors.

*44) In June 1948...two months after the
Italian election and the bogotazo, the one-year-
old National Security Council concluded that
these events meant the Soviet Union had launched
a vicious campaign against the United States. And
a secret directive was issued (approved by President
Truman) giving the CIA more power than ever before—allowing it now to engage in propaganda,
economic warfare, and preventive direct action,
evacuation measures, subversion against hostile
states, and assistance to underground resistance movements, guerrillas, and refugee liberation groups. These clandestine ops would be
planned and executed so that U.S. Government
responsibility wouldn't be evident, and, if uncovered, the U.S. Government could plausibly dis-
claim responsibility.*

— *from: "The Brothers—John Foster Dulles,
Allen Dulles, and Their Secret World War,"
by Stephen Kinzer*

45) *From "The Science of Coercion,"'*
by Christopher Simpson:

> *Basically all the heads of major media corporations were former OSS (the Office of Strategic Services, a U.S. intelligence agency during WWII) psychological warfare experts. That's a vital element of Cold War history that people forget. The media is basically waging psychological warfare against the public to get us to support America's foreign policy. They make you think that America is just trying to defend itself and that aggressors are coming out from everywhere. But the facts of the Cold War are that America was the aggressor and the Soviets were just scared of facing another invasion.'*

Fast forward to the Sandinista victory.

Desperate to meet the needs of its severely deprived populace, and with U.S. products no longer available, the Sandinistas gratefully accepted aid and trade from all willing countries, including nearby Cuba. Russia, too, a country of vast resources, was a willing trader.

But, in the U.S. playbook, trading with Commies confirmed Marxist leanings in the Sandinista ideology, (even though it was the U.S. embargo that pushed Nicaragua into new trade agreements; previously Nicaragua had been fine trading with us). For

Nicaragua Story

the U.S., this was precisely the rationale needed to 'protect' the Western Hemisphere more aggressively.

In fact, if the U.S. had its druthers, it would simply squash Nicaragua's new Sandinista government— that approach had worked nicely elsewhere. But there was a problem this time: the post-Vietnam, anti-war climate in the U.S. made it out of fashion (thus out of the question) to declare war on little Nicaragua and send down the troops.

So it looked like the Sandinistas would have to be eliminated some other way....

It's called guerrilla warfare—infiltrate and attack from within. Such would be the nature of the Contra War, from beginning to end.

> *46) Because the American people did not want another Vietnam on their hands, the United States' involvement with Nicaragua became frowned upon towards the end of the Somoza regime. Historians acknowledge that, for a short while, therefore, the Carter administration, then the Reagan administration, supported CIA back-door dealings with the Contras. Among the aid given to Contra militants were weapon caches and helicopters smuggled through the black market, plus covert money from the sale of arms to Iran—so the United States could fight its proxy war against Nicaragua without traceable evidence.*
>
> *The CIA also orchestrated covert Marine missions into Nicaragua and neighboring Hondu-*

ras to a) train the Contras, b) place mines in the Nicaraguan countryside, and c) get intel to the militants in the field once an actual civil war was underway in Nicaragua.

Though Americans themselves weren't tactically fighting this war against Nicaragua's socialist government, American-made bullets from American-made guns were killing Nicaraguans. And Ronald Reagan, then president, had made the demise of the Nicaraguan government an explicit aim of his foreign policy.

— from the book, "At War with Nicaragua,"
by Richard Ullman (from "CourseHero.com"
"The United States' Involvement in Nicaragua")

⁂

Was the U.S. justified at all? What was going on in Nicaragua?

47) The international development organization Oxfam explained the true reasons (from its experience of working with 76 developing countries): "The Sandinista government was exceptional in its commitment to improving the condition of the people and encouraging their active participation." Of the four Central American countries where Oxfam had a significant presence—El Salvador, Guatemala, Honduras,

*and Nicaragua—only in Nicaragua was there
a substantial effort to extend health, education,
and agricultural services to poor peasant families and to address inequities in land ownership.*

*And the World Bank, in the early 1980s,
said its projects were "extraordinarily successful
in Nicaragua, better than anywhere else in the
world."*

*As Jose Figueras, the father of Costa Rican
democracy, put it, "For the first time, Nicaragua
has a government that cares for its people."
Though Figueras was the leading democratic
figure in Central America for forty years, his
insights about the region were completely cen-
sored from U.S. media.*

— from: 'What Uncle Sam Really Wants,'
by Noam Chomsky, 2002

48) The fact was, the Sandinistas' successful reforms terrified the U.S. Secretary of State
George Shultz, who called the Sandinista government "a cancer right here on our land mass, trying to spread itself through various means."

— United Press International (UPI.com),
Feb. 27, 1986

49) That the Sandinistas could be so hated
for actually succeeding in directing resources to

*the poor was wondrous to behold. Almost all U.S.
policy makers shared that hatred, and it reached
a virtual frenzy.*

> *— from: "What Uncle Sam Really Wants,"
> "The Contra War in Nicaragua,"
> by Noam Chomsky, 2002*

The Sandinista government, led by President
Daniel Ortega and his cabinet, presented as friendly,
accessible, transparent, compassionate, and visionary.
Though many from the 'bourgeoisie' class, who'd supported the Somoza regime, scrambled from Nicaragua to
preserve their wealth (relocating mostly to the US), the
poor people stayed. And, for the first time in their history, had caring leaders with open and earnest policies,
instituting changes for the better.

But just when Nicaragua was poised to immeasurably improve life for its citizenry, all resources had to be
diverted into an undeclared, covert war, perpetrated by
the greatest force in the world. [50]

> *50) Historians now agree the U.S. went
> too far in trying to protect its borders from com-
> munist influence, and did so through shady, il-
> legal means.*
>
> *Discussed even more than the illegal aid
> the U.S. provided the Contras at that time are Am-
> erica's criminal practices pertaining to internation-*

al law. In the early 1980s, Nicaragua attempted to stop U.S. involvement within its borders by opening a case in the International Court of Justice. And Nicaragua won. Based on Article Two from the Charter of the United Nations, the ruling requested the U.S. cease intervention within Nicaragua's borders and observe basic principles of international law. Article Two states: "All members shall refrain...from the threat or use of force against the...political independence of any state."

Despite this court-ruled violation of international laws, the American government continued its covert operations, undermining and sabotaging Nicaragua.

According to historians, these violations of international law constitute political crimes.

— from the book, "At War with Nicaragua," by Richard Ullman (from "CourseHero.com")

Part Six – The Miskitos

~ 12 ~

Screening of Journalists

Back in Managua, I went to the neighborhood police in my *barrio*, to apply for residency, so as not to have to leave the country when my current visa expires, sixty days from my arrival date. A many-tiered process, it seems designed to drive one either insane or back to one's country of origin.

Today's exercise involved a forty-five-minute walk, interrupted by a delicious corn drink, ending in a tiny office (shack) labeled *"MIGRACION"* (immigration) in a Managua suburb.

Inside, two Sandinista officials were at work as four or five individuals waited in chairs to be processed. When my turn came, a sweet-looking young man perused my assorted credibility requirements: press card, letter from a U.S. newspaper, and Nicaraguan press ID. After carefully examining the display, he told me flatly that I could not have Nicaraguan residency. I should have entered the country on a technical visa, he stated, not as a tourist.

"How was I supposed to know that in the airport?" I asked.

He said he didn't know but that's what I should've done. He seemed fixed and I couldn't understand why; my documentation fulfilled all the requirements. It made no sense that he'd turn me down. And why would a journalist ask for a technical visa? This may be the protocol here, and might have aided me in getting residency, but until now no one anywhere in all my researching about what I needed had mentioned a technical visa. (Had I known, of course I'd have obtained one.)

A bilingual bystander then played interpreter for a while, as I pleaded my case, but nothing changed. In lieu of an impending stalemate, the official conceded somewhat and instructed me to bring the supervisor from the Nicaraguan Press Office *with me* here to this little hole in the wall. That seemed far-fetched—like asking the CEO of CBS for a lift to the laundromat. Sure, it might conceivably work, but was unlikely to happen.

Going along with it because I had zero options, I asked the man to write an explanatory note for me to present to this supervisor. He complied by scribbling in Spanish on a scrap of paper then handing me the unconvincing summons: "Please present yourself at the police station with *Señora* Wendy Raebeck."

I retired to a chair to pack up my paperwork, mope a bit, and brace myself for the heat outside. The kind translator was standing nearby. "Why is he making it so difficult for me?" I asked her.

"Because you're a journalist," she replied.

"Oh-h-h…" it sank in.

"You might be on the wrong side," she said.

(At that time, I was as yet unaware of CIA infiltration of the press, and the sober truth that practically *all* mainstream American media here were—despite their residency visas and their sashaying about Managua out-classing everybody—the enemy. But I did know how non-existent true Nicaragua stories were in the mainstream up north; despite reporters from major U.S. papers falling all over each other at press conferences here.)

The man finished with another gringo, an elderly American lady with the Episcopal Church, and I approached him again.

"*Señor*," I began in my best Spanish, "is the problem because I'm a journalist?"

"Yes," he answered.

"*Señor*, I would like to bring you my articles about Nicaragua so you can read what I'm writing. In the U.S. it is difficult to find the truth about the war in the newspapers. The information favors the Contras. I've come here to write the truth about the Sandinistas. May I bring you my articles? They're in English but you can look at them."

He didn't smile or change his expression. "I am responsible here," he said, touching his chest. "Whoever gets residency here, and whatever they do here, I'm responsible for it, because I approve them." He was looking into my eyes, his own underscoring the gravity of his job.

"I appreciate how careful you are," I said sincerely, looking into the immigration worker's conflicted eyes. "It's *important* that you be very careful."

With no change of expression, the young man then opened his book, and step by step began the residency process for me.

I spent Wednesday doing errands with a Dutch woman I'd met called Marioca. She's a student spending six months in Santo Tomas, a village of 2000 people. Her field is tropical agriculture and she's working through the National Nicaraguan Women's Organization. She said she's the only gringo in Santo Tomas, a location treacherously close to on-going battles and only "safe" because it's a fair-sized town.

Living with a Nicaraguan family, Marioca works daily in a women's garden co-op—her role, to help organize the garden, produce new crops, and get a better yield. But, after just one month there, she feels there's little she can 'teach' these women. The system they already have functions as well as can be expected with no tools, no nothing. "But just the fact that I'm there is an inspiration to them," she said; "that someone has come from somewhere else to work with them, and that the international community recognizes their struggle." So Marioca sees herself more as a support person, a helper, an international connection between these fifteen remote peasant women of the co-op and women elsewhere. She then told me how the women, all with children, are just now gaining confidence with their reading and writing skills, that they're all still learning the very basics. "So much of what goes on at the co-op has to do with personal growth as well as the growth of vegetables."

With regard to the war, Marioca was relieved to be in Managua "where there's no war." She said, "In Santo Tomas, it's right there, right outside the town. It used to be fifteen to twenty kilometers away, but it's closing in. Now the fighting's five to ten kilometers from the town."

"Are you ever afraid?"

"No," she said. "It's odd, but I don't think about it. Maybe if I did I'd be afraid."

~ October 3, 1986, Managua

~ 13 ~

Meeting at the Airport

My absentee husband, meanwhile, remained in
Montreal. This was years before the internet, so communication was either by letter (so slow that we didn't
bother) or phone. Phoning meant slogging forty-five
minutes in the broiling sun to the telecommunications
office (TelCor) to place the long-distance call. And this
after ferreting out TelCor's impossible-to-guess hours/
days of operation, then praying ferreted datum was
accurate and that some unforeseen interruption—someone having a baby, a bomb dropping, the lock on the
door being broken, or just nobody there for no reason—
hadn't affected the day's schedule. Then came the exor-
bitant fee for the call, and crossing my fingers Michel
would be home. If not, I could wait around in hopes of
more luck later, or return on whatever future day and
time the handwritten note on TelCor's door suggested.

About once a week I'd perform this ritual and
usually got through, to hurriedly exchange details and
devotion with the bridegroom. But, as time passed and
Michel still couldn't provide an ETA, I began wondering
if he was coming at all. Under my pleading, he'd then

cough up a date, that I'd look eagerly forward to, then hitch out to the airport on said day to throw my arms around him. But he wouldn't be on the plane! And I'd hitch dejectedly back to town.

As I labored to identify the root of the hold-up, Michel repeatedly assured me he was coming, "just not quite yet." But he still hadn't arranged any work down here to pay his way, and weeks were rolling by.

Did his chain of delays stem from the broken-arm handicap? Or was the guy on a totally different page? *Michel, hello-o! there's a war on down here!*

But this hubby wasn't someone I knew particularly well. And the relationship-slash-marriage was hardly on a predictable trajectory—Nicaragua, Mexico City, Venice, Vegas, Death Valley (our one-day honeymoon), Montreal, New York, now back to the war zone…. And it was disheartening having our long-awaited Nicaragua return without him, and continually stuffing disappointment into my backpack.

After nearly a month of false hopes, I uploaded my frustration into the phone. "Michel, you're missing everything. And I'm weary of waiting. There are places I need to go, I have work to do, and I've got to get going! If you're coming, COME, and if you're not, then DON'T."

∽✕∾

The other evening, I was at the airport (for a change) putting a U.S.-bound newspaper article on a flight, through a Costa Rican official (who I truly suspect is a Contra). Though a calculated risk, finding a personal courier to transport stories to a U.S. mailbox is, by far, the most expedient way to file articles. Afterwards, awaiting another of Michel's unvetted arrivals, I walked to the curb at the far end of the parking lot where palms in the afternoon breeze offered shade in which to sit and write. A few observant Sandinista guards left me alone.

Twenty minutes into scribbling on my clipboard, a skinny Nicaraguan man wandered over. I flashed a look of disinterest that he took as encouragement, and he moved closer. "I'm as sad as you," he said in mournful English, plunking himself down two inches away.

"I'm not sad," I said, and stood to go.

"I'm very sad," he continued, head in hands now.

"And very drunk," I added.

"Yes. I sorry. I sorry you should meet me like this. I was drinking a lot of beer. But I lost my keys. Oh, this is so bad. Have you seen any keys?"

"No…. Do you want me to help you look for them? Are they around here?"

He was about 58 or 60 and kind of a cute old guy.

"No, they're not here. They're lost. Oh no, this is so bad."

"Well, there's no point in moaning about it, let's look for them. Where'd you last see them, in the bar?"

"Maybe. Oh, I sorry you meet me like this. I'm head of my community, you know. I'm the leader. This is bad…."

"Which community?"

"Puerto Cabecas. I'm very important. Look, here's lots of documents with my name on them." He opened his leather briefcase and flashed typed pages covered with legal stamps and seals. Pointing to his name, in paragraphs here and there, he said, "Jacob Frances Warman, that's me...and that's me, and that's me. All me."

"Why don't you look in that bag for your keys, too?"

"They're not there."

"Just look."

He dug around superficially and found no keys.

Learning he was from Puerto Cabecas, a coastal town in the remote northeast region, about which I knew little, I had to ask, "What do you think about the revolution, about the Sandinistas?"

"We hate the Sandinistas," he hissed. "We *hate* them."

"Why?"

"They take everything. They selfish, dirty people."

"Do many people in Puerto Cabecas feel like you do?"

"Oh yes, everybody. All Indians hate them. All. They destroy everything."

"But was it better before, under Somoza?"

"Oh," his voice became dreamy, "Somoza was a gentleman. Somoza had dignity. These Sandinistas are a dirty people. Dirty."

"What do you mean? What do they do?"

"They control everything. They take everything. Before, we do as we like, live as we like. If you want to fish, you fish. Now everything is for them. The fish, they take all. Everything is for them."

"Do they pay for the fish?"

"Oh, they pay," he said accusingly, "but they take it ALL."

"But what about the Contra? Isn't it necessary to have Sandinistas there to protect you from the Contra?"

He looked at me strangely. "The Contra don't touch us. Never. They know. They *know.*"

"I thought it was extremely dangerous up in that region."

"Not for us."

"But I've read that the Contra kill people up there all the time."

"They only kill Sandinistas. Not us."

"They don't kill Indians?"

"No, they know. We are with them."

"Really?"

"Oh yes."

"Well, what do you think will happen in the future? This situation sounds very bad."

"It is the worst situation. The best thing that could happen would be an American invasion."

"An American invasion?"

"Yes."

"Why?"

"The only hope for us is if the Yankees wipe out the Sandinistas."

"But there will be a lot of blood."

"We are prepared to die, so our children can have a better life. It is the only hope." [51]

Whew...what an earful.

~ October 5, 1986, Managua

❧

51) — from The Washington Post,
Opinion Section, March 28, 1982
(author not given):

"The Use and Abuse of the Miskito Indians"

...The Nicaraguan government defends its systematic and heinous assault on the Miskitos on the grounds that the Indians are being used for CIA covert operations against the Sandinistas. The isolation of the northeast coast, it is argued, makes Miskito territory an inviting beachhead for counter-revolutionary American and Somozista attacks. The Nicaragua government and its supporters defend the forced relocation and the burning of Miskito villages, stating the Indians are being moved (at gunpoint) for their own protection, as well as for that of the 'revolution.'

Although the stark facts about the destruction of Miskito economy and culture are not disputed, the debate over the Indians' fate does not center on their right to stay on their land, to determine their own future, or to exist as a distinct people—it focuses on whether the CIA is planning covert action, whether it's recruiting Indian mercenaries, or whether the killing of 20 or 60 Sandinista soldiers justifies massive Indian removal.

From a human rights perspective, this is an unconscionable and cynical argument, in which being a victim of CIA abuse and manipulation entitles the Miskitos to further drastic abuse by the Sandinistas. It is an argument that premises Miskito survival on the readiness of Washington to refrain from sacrificing them in a global power-play.

The actual policies of both the U.S. and Nicaraguan governments show their fundamental disregard for the human rights of the Miskito people, despite their protestations of concern. The U.S. decries Sandinista attacks on the Miskito, while itself using the Indians as pawns to keep the world safe for democracy—knowing the suffering their actions will inflict on the Indians. The Sandinistas, on the other hand, use U.S. covert operations and military threats from Honduras as a pretext for their policy of 'forced assimilation,' planned long before these current military problems.

Relocating the Miskitos isn't a temporary emergency measure but a long-planned resettlement "for the development of the Atlantic coast" and for "improving and dignifying the living con-

ditions of the Miskitos." (*Each Indian family re-moved from its homeland will be given a 250-square-meter piece of private property.*)

It is urgent that organizations committed to human rights intervene through negotiations and physical presence to prevent the destruction of yet another indigenous people.

~ 14 ~

Inadequacies

With his hot little honey losing faith, Michel realized the sands of our joint venture were running out. After my ultimatum, he stopped waffling, emptied his piggy bank, and boarded a plane. The purse strings would be tight, and the plan had never been for him to be my sidekick, but I could use a helper and he would prove to be that in spades—a born supporter, embued with skills, and a technical genius.

Michel felt inadequate having no work in Nicaragua, especially while foregoing jobs back home, but marriage takes sacrifice and he was being a great husband. Though we'd have to skimp a bit in our peregrinations and day-to-day kerfuffles, all would actually be more streamlined not juggling two workloads.

Being in each other's arms again and resuming our stride as a sturdy pair was long overdue. And, in contrast to the misfortune surrounding us in Nicaragua, we felt more than lucky in every way.

Today, however, our coupledom almost dissolved over the difficulties of just extricating ourselves from Managua.

Trying to get residency here, and now a visa extension in the meantime — because I belatedly discovered that Americans only get thirty days upon arrival where other foreigners get sixty — is so infuriating, time consuming, and rigged with snares requiring you to repeat the whole process, that I almost surrendered my sanity. In the Press Office yesterday — third visit there in two days and not the last — I said, "How am I supposed to do any of the work I'm requesting residency for, like *journalism*, when ALL my time goes into fulfilling endless requirements?"

I can't even think about all the stomping around still to be done in Managua. And now they tell me that once I finish the residency application, I have to wait thirty days to get the permit! While my plane ticket back to the States expires.

I have no desire to go back to the States (ever), but my sub-letter's leaving November 8th. So…instead of pushing to do all the steps faster somehow, we've vacated the blasted town! I have four more articles to write in the next thirty days and need to be out in the countryside talking to *campesinos* and taking pictures, not enmeshed in bureaucracy.

The main reason to establish residency before leaving is so I don't have to re-apply for extensions every time I return, plus pay $60 each time. And leaving without residency could seriously mean never getting back here…since it's *so* trying generating the funds for these missions. With residency, at least I could hurdle recurring expenses and the endless red tape. Plus, I've already done so much of the footwork at this point that it's worth completing.... But it's getting sticky.

✑

All I know with certainty is I have to keep working.

Ergo, with heat oppressive and bags heavy, Michel and I stood on the roadside with only a flimsy belief we'd feel better outside the city. Heading east toward Chaquitillo and Matagalpa, we extended our thumbs. After a flurry of short rides, we lucked out when a nurse from San Francisco in a station wagon took us all the way to the Sebaco junction.

This nurse, her husband, and their fifteen-year-old daughter are spending a year working in a clinic up north in Estelí, near the Honduran border. Back in the States, while fundraising for their program here, a friend had suggested they ask singer Jackson Browne to help. That friend had met Browne here last year at one of the weekly Thursday morning demonstrations in front of the American Embassy in Managua. So the couple sent the rock star an explanatory letter, heard nothing for months, then one morning got a call from Jackson himself saying he'd arranged a benefit concert in San Francisco for them and three other Central American war-related causes. [52]

Now here they were.

52) *On several trips to Nicaragua, Jackson Browne, the 39-year-old singer-song-writer was struck by what he called "the serenity of a loving people." He said, "War has pulled them closer in a way that consumeristic Americans might find difficult to comprehend."*

...Political protest came to the fore in Browne's music in the 1986 album, "Lives in the Balance," an explicit condemnation of U.S. policy in Central America. It was a huge success with Browne fans, though not with mainstream audiences. The title track, "Lives in the Balance," was an outcry against U.S.-backed wars in Nicaragua, El Salvador, and Guatemala.

— Wikipedia

'There's a shadow on the faces
Of the men who fan the flames
Of the wars that are fought in places
Where we can't even say the names' 53

53) *These lyrics were used in the award-winning 1987 PBS documentary: "The Secret Government: The Constitution in Crisis," by journalist Bill Moyers.*

— Wikipedia

Nicaragua Story

On Nicaraguan radio, Jackson Browne's song,
"Wake Up, America," plays all the time:

"Voice of America"

sung by Jackson Browne in 1986
(Original song by Little Steven.
Browne sang it as a cover.)

Can you hear me? Wake up!
Where's the voice of America?
Somebody help me, we gotta stop a crime
I been betrayed by my own kind
I been quiet, too quiet
While across the borderline
We die

Can you hear me? Wake up!
Where's the voice of America?
I know that we knew right from wrong once upon a time
Everything we stood for has been compromised
I been quiet, too quiet
While across our borderline
My people lie

Can you hear me? Wake up!
Where's the voice of America?
You're quiet, too quiet
Are you still alive
Inside

Can you hear me? Wake up!
We're the voice of America
We're the voice of America
We're the voice of America
We're the voice of America

~ *October 8, 1986, Chaquitillo*

~ 15 ~

Jarred Perspective

Jacob Frances Warman, the Indian chief, jarred my perspective. Though brimming with bitterness and beer, he still represented a huge group of people, the Miskito Indians.

Like most foreigners here, I'd been swept up in the overriding viewpoints on this side, the Pacific, for the simple reason that the Atlantic/Caribbean side is so separate — no connecting road (through dense jungle), different languages, different culture, different history, and no participation in the politics of a revolution emanating exclusively from Managua.

But was Nicaragua actually two disparate countries?

We gringos in the western/Spanish portion of Nicaragua had never denied there could be differing sentiments on the eastern/Atlantic side. (And, of course, the U.S. press had made an issue of it.) But we were ensconced in the ideology of the Sandinistas, their humanitarian goals for raising everyday standards, achieving equity for all, and eliminating scar tissue from the endless reign of terror that had so polarized rich and poor. The Sandinista dreams and their success in leading the people were stimulating and impressive. And the vision surged onward with the vast majority of people in solidarity...over on the 'Spanish' side of the country.

But, being down here as a writer and a concerned American, this 'problem' of the Miskitos becomes my problem. To have written so much about Nicaragua, and nothing about the Miskitos, makes me now feel a victim of revolutionary fervor. And to try to somehow visit the Miskitos' region becomes urgent.

True, the Sandinista Revolution has grown out of this side of the country, just as the government is here, the Somoza regime was based here, the capital is here, and the impetus is here...but it's frightening. And terrifying. Because if there's any correlation between these cowboys and Indians and the ones we Americans watched on TV throughout our childhoods, then I've been on the wrong side in Nicaragua....

I know I'm jumping to hasty conclusions about which I know little. In no way are the Sandinistas wiping out the Indians or wishing to eliminate them. The question is, can European and Indian cultures *ever* co-exist? If so, how? Looking at North American history, one could deduce that the Indian way of life might have served the land and the politics of Americans far better than the cowboy culture that obliterated it. But the cowboys won because they had gunpowder. And American politics have never really abandoned the ideology that 'we can beat you physically'...'and we will if you mess with us.'

Here, the Sandinistas have gunpowder. But they're of Spanish heritage. It's the Indians who are the *natives of this land.*

But the plot thickens even more when it comes to the Contra. They may well be sparing Indians, even

courting an alliance with them — but hardly for the sake
of the Indians' well-being!

Is anyone really on the side of the Indians?

Or, are the Meskitos, too, doomed to be another
embarrassment in history books? [54 & 55]

~ *October 10, 1986, Jinotega*

*54) Never close to the central government,
the Miskitos began to actively oppose the Sandinistas in 1982 when authorities killed more than a
dozen Indians, burned villages, forcibly recruited
young Miskito men into the Army and tried to re-
locate others. Thousands of Miskitos then poured
across the border into Honduras, and many took
up U.S.-supplied arms to oppose the Nicaraguan
government.*

*Their struggle has always been separate
from the main Contra forces. The Miskitos say they
are fighting for autonomy for their homeland, but
they do not trust the main Contra group to grant
them that, were the Contra to ever gain power.*

*55) The Miskitos did not fit into the San-
dinistas' schema of a society composed of capita-
lists and workers. The implication was that Miskitos were a dinosaur-like relic that moderniza-
tion—either capitalist or socialist—would sweep
away, the sooner the better.*

*...In building a new sovereign nation in
the face of imperialism, it was not difficult to*

view groups such as native peoples, that weren't involved in rebellion against capitalism, as a symbol of backwardness.

But, in light of all this, it's understandable that the Miskitos began to fight for their rights.

It's also been suggested that, on some deeper level, the Northeast jungles of the Atlantic Coast were as foreboding to the Sandinistas as they were to the original Conquistadors— mysterious, unknown, and treacherous.

Studying the Sandinista-Miskito conflict without prejudice is a necessary first step in preventing misunderstandings in the future.

> — "Miskitos and Sandinistas"
> by L. Proyect, Columbia University
> (no date given)

Part Seven – Dire Straits

~ 16 ~

Always More to the Story

Michel and I arrived in Chaquitillo and followed the dirt road to Eric's modest structure with the earthen-floor kitchen, wood-burning stove, and outhouse. He bought it for $1000, and lives congenially between two other identical dwellings, containing twenty or so members of two Nicaraguan families. We found him making a wooden door for a family down the road, with a team of young boys apprenticing around him.

Spending the night at Eric's was both inspiring and radically unsettling. Eric, like most foreigners here, is genuinely helping these hard-working people in a time of cataclysmic need. After participating in several brigades and living in different parts of the western regions of the country, he's settled in Chaquitillo as a kind of resident saint. Non-stop every day, he assists the community. Anything he can acquire — t-shirts, cucumbers, Chinese herbal diarrhea medicine — he scores in bulk. Then he either dashes from house to house distributing the goods or holds court in his living room as word circulates that he's got stuff. Or that he's making a vat of soup. Tonight it's gringos with balloons. (Michel brought some from Canada.) It takes about thirty seconds for the first arrivals to show, then a stream of consumers continues until bedtime or until Eric runs out of steam. If the commodity du jour runs out, he hands out something else—coloring books, pencils. In a land of almost nothing material, anything you can see and touch is treasured.

Powerhouse Eric also farms acres of land nearby and has planted vegetables the Nicaraguans don't customarily grow. The concept is to introduce 'new' foods like eggplant and okra by liberally distributing them. Then, when the harvest is over, Eric gives everybody seeds so they can grow the crops themselves.

A big-hearted eccentric supported by wealthy, politically minded parents in California, Eric is forty-three, lives on garden food, and is rapidly becoming the godfather of tiny Chaquitillo. His humble domain has luxuries like tools, a stereo, a blender, all in constant use accommodating one and all. He's made all his own furniture, and plenty for other people. He also works on the construction of a daycare center a New York brigade is building up the road.

But Michel and I were to discover more to Eric's profile.

His magnanimity is thrown violently into question by his interaction with the little neighbor girls.

While the six-year-olds were at his table, absorbed in their magical coloring books—standing on either side of where Eric was seated — Michel and I were flabbergasted to see his hands sliding up their legs.

And, as is frequently the case, the children pretended nothing was happening.

Eric didn't even conceal what he was doing from Michel and I, seated right there with him at the table. And good ol' Bart, also in the room, was equally unruffled. (As Eric's revolutionary roadie for years, this behavior couldn't be news to him.)

Sickened, Michel and I didn't know what to do. In our side-by-side sleeping bags a while later, we whispered about actions we could take, but knew we had no proof, inadequate Spanish, and that Eric would likely deny it. [56]

> 56) With today's zero tolerance for sexual predators, we surely would've reported Eric to neighboring families and the police. Back then, though, child molestation was completely under wraps, considered bizarre, and even perverse to talk about. Incidences of it were so undisclosed that the subject was taboo. So Michel and I, though appalled and ashamed for every person in the room, were also confused...because Eric was, in other ways, the best thing that ever happened to this war-impoverished village.
>
> A few weeks later, however, we learned that he'd been kicked out of the Architects and Planners Brigade. Our friends up there wouldn't

*say why, nor wish to discuss it—again, child abuse
was unacknowledged—but they'd booted him from
their brigade. And we knew why.*

Next morning, excusing ourselves from the
swarming kids begging for everything in sight, Eric took
us to the daycare center the gringos were constructing. It
was ample and awesome with its own sewer system and
space for a generous garden. These projects add promise
and encouragement to small communities like Chaquitillo. Imagine what a free daycare center would mean to a
community anywhere!

We then hiked up a stone canyon to check out
Mayan rock carvings Eric knew of. Then, walking back
from the hills, a farmer friend of Eric's, Juan Garcia,
passed in his pick-up and invited us out to his land. Eric
was delighted since the farm visit would mean half a
truckload of free veggies for his "family." And Michel
and I were game for anything.

I could see by the rapport Juan Garcia had with
his two dogs that he was a gem. And for the next two
hours, with Michel and Eric in back with the pups,
Juan and I chatted in the cab of the truck. I posed my
standard question straight away, *"Que piense de la guerra?"*
("What do you think about the war?") This ungarnished
query invoked frank and personal accounts from everyone I encountered.

"It's a very serious situation," Juan regarded me
from under his low hat. "Very grave. It's not a war between the U.S. and Russia, it's a civil war. But the U.S.
and Russia are fighting it with our soldiers."

"A civil war?"

"Yes, I know a woman up in Jinotega who has five sons—three are Contras, two are Sandinistas."

As a large land owner, Juan Garcia had some insecurities about the Sandinistas, believing his land could be taken from him. On the other hand, he wasn't against their good intentions. His main concerns were that the war made it impossible to get equipment and that money was so tight. "A few years ago, a man could earn two dollars a day;" he shook his head, "now it's two dollars a week. The exchange rate used to be seven *cordobas* for a dollar; now it's two thousand *cordobas* for a dollar."

~ October 11, 1986, Jinotega

~ 17 ~

Headline News

My third arrival in Matagalpa was as pleasant as the first two—verdant hills hugging the town, faded hues and quaint vistas captivating from every angle. I'm content just rambling through the village. Shop doors are open, folks on business zig-zag across streets, the breeze is cool, and all is vivid despite afternoon rains. [57]

> 57) *The scars of war are evident. Shelves in many shops, pharmacies in particular, are almost empty, store windows sometimes comical with only one or two items—a pair of brown plastic sandals and a tube of lipstick. Inside the stores are odd assortments: underpants, hammocks, combs and ketchup…whatever they can get.*
>
> *— LA Weekly, "Other Places," May 2, 1986, by Wendy Raebeck*

Michel appreciated Matagalpa, though was struck by the quantity of soldiers everywhere. But, as one moves closer to toward *el Frente* (the Front), the

numbers must increase. Here, Sandinistas are sta-
tioned even atop the hills.

Of course all the hotels were packed, and we
had to settle into a real kennel. There was no sink
anywhere in the establishment. They didn't even have
waste baskets in the bathrooms for the newspaper
(toilet paper rarely exists beyond Managua). The noise
level was off the charts because two extra beds were
in the hall outside our chamber, that, per usual, didn't
have walls reaching the ceiling. The courtyard was
mud. So when you went to the bathroom, you came
back filthy. Okay, fair enough, we're in a war; but the
so-called management couldn't even provide a bent nail
on the outhouse door, that didn't properly close. So
you had to hold it closed with your foot when you sat.
But if you preferred not to sit, the obvious preference,
you had to let the door swing open. And this facility
was situated directly across from the main entrance.

The next day, this same management took a
coffee break at noon—seconds after we'd paid and
said we were leaving in five minutes—and locked us in
the courtyard during their absence. When the young
woman came lolly-gagging back, I told her plainly that
it was *muy malo* (very bad) to lock guests in the hotel.

In no accounts about the revolution have I
read anything about the level of disintegration here.
I even hesitate to photograph the true conditions. It's
an impossible country to visit other than for work or
conducting research—just getting from place to place
is, at best, a huge effort. But, not having been here ten
years ago, it's hard to ascertain which direction it's all

going. Sometimes Nicaragua seems to be spinning into chaotic despair, other times returning from there. It's as easy to hate the place as love it. But it's difficult for everyone.

Being away from Managua, we missed the giant drama of the Contra C-123 cargo transport plane shot down. All the attention surrounding this is in Managua and I should be scratching around down there for the story, but it was not mentally possible to return to that madhouse after just one day out. I called the *LA Weekly* to find out what news is coming through in the U.S. and not one of the four editors I asked for was in. (I even learned that the one who'd commissioned me to send back stories had been let go!)

So maybe I'll write a follow-up piece about the cargo plane a bit later. Anyway, I'm not responsible for breaking news, am not a reporter, not on salary. I'm a freelancer, on my own dime, writing my own stories.

But the Nicaraguan press has had a field day over this; front page news for three days straight. The first two days, there was nothing else at all in any paper except stories and photos of the cargo handler Eugene Hasenfus, the crashed plane, and the three young Sandinistas responsible for the capture. Hasenfus was the sole survivor of the crash. The three other men aboard, two of whom were American, were killed.
58, 59, 60 & 61

58) In October 1986, a plane flown by
Eugene Hasenfus, carrying military equipment

intended for the Contras, was shot down over Nicaragua. The Reagan administration publicly denied that Hasenfus sought to arm the Contras as part of a U.S. government mission. However, the State Department was centrally involved in the covert plan to fund the Contras, which violated congressional legislation. In congressional testimony in October 1986, Elliott Abrams (Assistant Secretary of State) repeatedly and categorically denied that the US government was involved in arming the Contras. However, at the time, Abrams knew that Oliver North was encouraging, coordinating, and directing the activities of the Contra re-supply, and that North was in contact with the private citizens behind the lethal re-supply flights.

During the later investigation of the Iran-Contra Affair, Abrams admitted that he knew more than he acknowledged in his congressional testimony, and entered a plea agreement.

— *Wikipedia*

59) Given the Reagan Administration's anti-Gaddafi disinformation campaign, one may be skeptical of the Administration's denials of U.S. government support or involvement for the C-123 transport plane that was shot down by the Nicaraguan military.

The questions now become when will President Reagan send a letter to Nicaraguan President Daniel Ortega assuring him that the captured American Eugene Hasenfus is not a CIA spy, and for whom will Secretary of State George Shultz trade Hasenfus?

— *LA Times, October 14, 1986*

60) The Sandinista People's Tribunal trying Eugene Hasenfus is expected to hand down a verdict and sentence Friday or Monday. "The question of whether to pardon will be a later decision by Nicaraguan President Daniel Ortega," said Foreign Ministry spokesman Angla Saballow. It was indicated today that Nicaragua might pardon Hasenfus for his role in supplying the U.S.-backed Nicaraguan rebels with weapons.

— *LA Times, November 13, 1986*

61) Eugene Hasenfus, the American air cargo handler captured when his arms-laden plane was shot down over Nicaragua in October, confessed that he had been smuggling weapons to anti-government (Contra) Nicaraguan rebels. Tried by a Nicaraguan People's Tribunal, his sentence of a thirty-year jail term was the maximum allowed under Nicaraguan law.

Today, however, Mr. Hasenfus was pardoned and freed. He was turned over to Senator Christopher Dodd, Democrat of Connecticut, and left Nicaragua aboard a jet with Mr. Dodd.

At a news conference in Nicaragua, President Daniel Ortega announced, "We are turning citizen Hasenfus over to the American people." Mr. Ortega said he hoped the pardon would "contribute to ending once and for all the criminal war that has been imposed on us." And he said American political and religious leaders who oppose U.S. policy toward Nicaragua had urged a pardon.

In Washington, the State Department said it was pleased at Mr. Hasenfus's release, but said, "The handling of this entire incident was orchestrated by the Sandinistas for maximum propaganda effect. The fundamental totalitarian nature of the Sandinista regime has not changed, and our policy toward Nicaragua has not changed."

— NY Times, December 18, 1986

~ 18 ~

Florita

To get closer to the Front, we had to go up to Jinotega, the last town before the jungly mountains of the northeast part of the country. I absolutely needed to verify that the through-road to Puerto Cabecas on the east coast was closed to all but military. I'd been told this by knowledgeable sources, but things can change....

We left Matagalpa next afternoon, intending to thumb the forty kilometers north. But dozens of others shared our agenda, all coagulated at a bus stop on the edge of town—some futilely hitching, others banking on the bus. Waiting our turn for thumbing space, we spent hours by the roadside. At one jubilant moment, an incoming bus was spotted, but on arrival was so bursting with *pasajeros* that we couldn't possibly squeeze aboard with our packs. (I have to be vigilant about my work gear; vanishing cargo has been reported on these buses. With elbows and shoulders in your face, it's tough to guard equipment stashed three rows back under someone's seat.)

After several sweaty hours in the sun, we opted for any cab that would cram us in. One congenial driver lowered the price from 10,000 to 5,000 (or $5 to $2.50) for us, since everyone in the cab knew $5 was the gringo price and we didn't want to come off as *stupidos*.

Funny how you start thinking in nickels and dimes here. But where 'time is money' in North America, 'money is more time' for us down here. Regarding lodging, most Americans would say, "It's so cheap, let's stay in a nicer places," but a) nicer places only exist in Managua (somewhere, maybe), and b) we'd rather spend less on rooms and transport and eat better.

Halfway up the first mountain, the driver pulled over, grabbed some cloth from the glove compartment and a plastic burlap bag from under his seat, then, using the hood of the car as a work table, neatly rolled them up. What was he doing? Michel and I, along with the three *Nicas* in the back seat, observed in silence. The driver then placed this rolled-up lump between the two front bucket seats as a cushion so I wouldn't have to sit on the emergency brake. We all laughed. Then, grabbing his screwdriver from the dashboard, he started the engine again.

We continued on up to 5,000 feet, high into the lush, misty mountains. Everything was green, quiet, and remote. The road wound around and through, some turns affording fifty-mile views across valleys, ridges, and mountains fading into every hue of green, green, green. It was like Austria or Wales, sweet and unspoiled. When the rain started and it got cold, we were doubly glad not to be on top of a bus (where we'd have ended up had we stuck it out at the busstop).

Jinotega was chilly, wet, high in altitude, and not unlike other Nicaraguan towns in appearance (Matagalpa and Managua excepted) — flat, spread-out, and a sort of pastel disaster. Memories of old paint on every building. Like the rest of Nicaragua, residents here appeared to be a blend of polyester cowboys with Indian faces, and intense black-eyed women in blue eye shadow, stockings, and dime-store dresses. But stern faces in the streets turn to candy when you give them a smile.

I half hoped to run into Don, the guy who'd driven me in his Jeep back from Matagalpa to Managua last time. He's building a generator out in Cua, a resettlement community about 100 kilometers northeast of Jinotega. But the hearsay was correct, civilians may not travel those mountainous dirt roads to Cua or anywhere else without permission from the military. No cabs, buses, or personal vehicles may pass. As a journalist, I might've somehow obtained permission, but I'm careful out here — this is *not* a place to fly by the seat of your pants.

We didn't see Don. But we met a young woman named Laurie from Saskatchewan, Canada, one of only two or three gringos in the town. She'd hitched down from Condega, only 50 kilometers farther north, but she'd had to take a 150-kilometer detour south (four hours through Estelí, Sebaco, and Matagalpa) because the direct road was closed to all but military.

Laurie was in Nicaragua to help midwives and learn more about midwifery in the process. She'd been working two weeks in a clinic up in Condega with an American woman who was doing sometimes two births a day. But that woman was burning out and wouldn't be continuing much longer, so Laurie came to Jinotega hoping to volunteer with a Nicaraguan midwife she'd heard about here.

Leaving Michel to a quiet breakfast and newspaper, I accompanied Laurie on foot in search of that midwife, Florita, who we found at her home address.

Florita, about forty with a sparkling face, opened her door and, automatically, her home to us, before we said a word. Laurie hesitatingly explained the purpose of our visit, and practically before she finished, Florita was holding both Laurie's hands, stroking them, and whole-heartedly accepting her offer of help. She said Laurie was welcome to live in her house, too. And, in mere moments, had us both seated at a big table and served us heaping plates of lunch. It even turned out she'd delivered a baby the night before and the mother and infant were recuperating in her back room.

Florita then disappeared to dress for a funeral. As we ate and acknowledged Laurie's splendid fortune in meeting such a woman, and so easily, Florita's husband, Julio, joined us at the table. He spoke about Florita's work, how busy she was, and how terrific it was that Laurie could help. He said Florita also teaches classes on midwifery and birth control, to people in Jinotega as well as rural midwives from the countryside. "But the rural midwives can't risk coming down here for classes anymore," he said, "the roads are too dangerous. They can't even come to town for supplies.

And the same goes for pregnant women. Although a clinic birth in the town is considered safer than a home birth with no access to emergency equipment, it's now safer to birth at home than risk a Contra attack on the road to town."

Julio then solemnly told us that two days ago there'd been an attack fifteen kilometers away and his twenty-three-year-old nephew had been killed. The young man had been driving down the road, followed by a married couple on a motorcycle—the woman was seventeen and pregnant. All three were killed. The woman was slit from the chest straight down. The funeral was today.

"Twenty-three years old," Julio dropped his head.

Laurie and I couldn't finish our food. We just sat there.

The sorrow here is so commonplace. But you don't get used to it—the horror always theirs, never yours. You're sad, sick, guilty, and confused, yet grateful for your own well-being…all at the same time. But, most of all, as hard as you try to climb into their eyes or their hearts, you can't know the pain.

We walked with Florita and Julio toward the church. Their little terrier, Conga, couldn't be persuaded to stay home, though Florita knew his cheery demeanor was at odds with the service they'd be attending.

That evening, the town was heavy. The soldiers somber. There seemed more of them now than ever.

Our little Hotel Tito had a tiny restaurant that served
Cokes and milkshakes (milk with banana flavoring),
creating a local hang-out. Michel and I sat sipping
shakes around 8 o'clock, while the whole room and the
whole night felt black and swollen with fear and death.
The soldiers, so young in their olive garb, finished their
Cokes. No one had much to say. Their huge trucks were
parked out front in the rain. In moments, they'd climb
back into them and go….

Go where? Up into the hills to guard the town
and the roads, or out into some valley maybe where
there was fighting. Maybe they'd go to live in a tent for
a month, or go guard a bridge. Maybe they'd go sit on
top of a summit and just watch the surrounding hills
day and night. One thing was certain, the Contra were
close.

In the forefront of everybody's mind now, too,
was this "Yankee" prisoner, Eugene Hasenfus. The
power behind the Contra, the immensity of it and the
heartlessness, was more shrill than ever. The responsibility of these Sandinista soldiers ever greater to try to
stop it.

Once we'd learned we couldn't continue north or
east with the roads closed, we were okay heading back
to Managua. Plenty to do there, with the residential visa
hoopla. And I needed to look into the Hasenfus incident. We also wanted to get permission for an east coast
trip to Bluefields, via that bus-boat itinerary.

We sat by the road next morning for about an
hour, but there was no traffic. Just other hitchers of

every shape and size. But suddenly a loaded bus lum-
bered in. There was no one on the roof, no one falling
out the doors, so we tried to flag it down since we
weren't on a bus-stop. Since it was going so slowly it
was practically in reverse, it stopped for us. To our
elation, it was going all the way to Managua!

The ride cost 10 cents each, plus a 40-cent fee
for all our baggage. And when numerous passengers
alighted in Matagalpa, we even scored seats.

~ *October 17, 1986, Managua*

~ 19 ~

Who's on Whose Side?

We two are biding time in Managua. Now conditioned to thinking in nickels and dimes, second-hand dictates of war and poverty, we've relocated to *Hospedaje* Chipitos, comparable to the Santos but half the price.

We've had several days of cloudiness and rain, characteristic of the final days of this season. All appreciate the coolness of the rains and regret the season ending. Taking it all in, I'm swilling a corn-and-milk drink at the shady stand across from the Immigration Office, that aforementioned shanty. On Wednesday they told me to come back Friday. It's Friday, here I am, and the place is locked up. "Today's a holiday," explained the lady at the drink stand.

"Then why did they tell me to come back Friday?"

"They didn't know it was a holiday."

'CLOSED FOR NO REASON' might be an accurate sign to post everywhere about half the time.

~ October 20, 1986, Managua

∞

With my zillion documents now in order, I obediently presented myself at the Press Center today only to be informed it'll take another two days to process everything. I almost wept. How am I supposed to write about the East Coast when stuck in Managua filing endless paperwork? I'd hoped to get my residency permit, fly back to the States, earn some money, then return here with far fewer visa hassles. Now—informed it will take *another full month* (while my plane ticket expires in three weeks)—I either have to be on that flight, scrapping all the headway I've made toward residency, or forfeit the ticket and stay here with no ticket back and little money.

"Forget the whole thing!" I said loudly, gathered my *documentos*, and headed for the door. But before leaving, I told the whole room—in rotten Spanish, and much to everyone's discomfort—that if they wanted the American public to understand the Nicaraguan situation better, they should make it possible for American journalists to do their work! And that I felt I'd been given an especially hard time because I'm from the U.S.

"There are lots of American journalists working here," the lady in the office replied curtly.

True. And true, too, that in addition to their resident visas, they all have cushy American salaries letting them live LARGE here and that's what they're doing. I felt like asking if anyone in this office had ever read what those journalists write. (I have.)

Oh well, I may not have the lavish income or the visa, but I do have my ally Michel standing by. And all that matters now is that I get to the East Coast quickly, before my flight, to write about the other 'side' of this country—meaning also 'the other side' of this war.

Hopefully we'll head out tomorrow.

~ *October 25, 1986, El Rama*

∾❀∾

After observing Petra's herculean efforts a few weeks back, preparing for that all-in-one-day endurance trial to Bluefields—first securing her ticket, then actually catching that singular bus from Managua to Rama the next day—Michel and I resolved to depart at a reasonable hour instead and just hitch-hike as far as the road goes (to El Rama). There, we could spend the night then catch the riverboat to the Atlantic coast the following day. Once in Bluefields, perhaps we'd even take another boat to Corn Island, supposedly a paradise. (Though the definition of 'paradise' has to be fairly diluted around here.) (Like maybe a bus with two empty seats.)

Because I had to attend the weekly demonstration in front of the American Embassy (the on-going protest) to connect with my latest courier to transport an article, Michel and I didn't even hoist our thumbs until one p.m. But, as previously mentioned, a trusted courier is a hot commodity. Plus, it was good to attend the demonstration. This group of Americans has protested every Thursday morning for three years! Today, 100 people participated, beside an erect line of soldiers guarding the already tightly secured Embassy building, hardly a sacred shrine here.

I walked to the protest with John, the Fulbright scholar who also lives in our *hospedaje*. To finance his participation in the revolution, i.e. his return to Nicaragua, he'd managed to win this scholarship by explaining to a board of directors (in impressive academic lingo) how he wanted to study Nicaraguan poetry. But he was then apprised that Fulbright scholars are managed by the same branch of the federal government that handles the CIA! [62]

> *62) In countries without a Fulbright Commission, but that have an active program, the Public Affairs section of the U.S. Embassy oversees the Fulbright Program.*
>
> — *Wikipedia*

So part of his requirement is to stay in close contact with the Embassy. He also had to sign a contract pledging he won't participate in any activities that go against U.S. interests. However, this arrangement has provided him direct access to the Embassy officials—a crowd generally scorned by other foreigners in Nicaragua. And John has unbridled access to both the Embassy and their club, "Casa Grande," an old mansion with a restaurant and pool.

Milking his position to see what he can sniff out, he's already determined that there's a good chance the Embassy and all its people will soon be pulling out of Managua. He's on the list of Americans to be flown out by the Embassy and has been told to check in regularly since he doesn't have a phone.

"Should this occur, it will happen quickly," John said. And he surmises that, shortly thereafter, Managua will be bombed.

"Gosh, John, you're in a good position," I said. "You should get a strong Sandinista contact, somebody high up, and let them know immediately if the Embassy people tell you they're leaving."

"I have a contact," he nodded.

"A solid person who can get the word right through to the Sandinista government?"

"Yes, a very solid contact."

Part Eight – Lives in the Balance

~ 20 ~

' Fe '

My *compadre* and I hit the street after lunch, hitching as far as Benito (not far), where allegedly there was a small bus to Juigalpa at 4 p.m. that, fortuitously, we caught. "It's 25 cents each…." warned the conductor. But we'd break the bank to keep moving and maybe get as far as Santo Tomas. There, I thought we might locate Marioca, the Dutch woman who works at the women's farm cooperative.

On the bus, I started chatting with a matronly Nicaraguan woman named Sedonia who spoke English fairly well and who gradually transitioned from aloof nonchalance to humorous warmth. About halfway to Juigalpa, she told us that this bus was only going as far as Acoyapa and it would be too dark by then to hitch to Santo Tomas. "You better stay at my house," she said. "Small house, big heart."

I realized how foolish we'd been to set out so late. You can't hitch at night out here because a) there's no traffic since the nighttime roads are too dangerous, and b) anyone on the road by necessity will not stop for *any* reason, lastly to pick up strangers!

So, we got off with Sedonia in Juigalpa and went to her home, where she was greeted by her four children and her mother. Sedonia and her husband both work Monday through Friday in Managua, two and a half hours from home, she as a biologist, he as a doctor. Adhering to this schedule for five years now, her mother cares for the kids Monday morning to Friday night.

Sedonia fed us a typical Nicaraguan meal of *gallopinto* (rice and beans), some old meat (that to be polite we had to eat), and hunks of white bread from the four large loaves she carried from Managua. Water was the beverage. Her youngest son joined us, nibbling on white bread with honey—seemingly his dinner. The Nicaraguan diet is frightening. Except for the corn tortillas, shredded cabbage sprinkled on meals, *frijoles* (beans), and fresh fruit, God knows how they make it. They all drink *refrescos* day and night—fresh fruit drinks loaded with sugar—and consume eye-popping quantities of white bread, stuffing their young with it.

After dinner, we stayed around the table talking about the Nicaraguan situation. Like so many of her country folk, Sedonia talked easily about her spirituality as integral to her life. Religion here helps many hang on in the face of so much death and difficulty. They believe in what they're doing as a people and as a nation. "Rightness is what our religion is based on," she told me, "doing what's right, no matter what the consequences."

This faith, or *fe* in Spanish, might well be the binding force of the revolution.

Throughout Central America, Catholicism is the predominant religion (by a long shot), and penetrates all aspects of life. I think you could safely generalize that Central Americans take their religion more seriously and literally than the majority of North Americans do. At the same time, there doesn't seem to be much questioning of what's passed down from the Catholic Church.... North Americans, under the banner of freedom, are more skeptical about doctrine. (Despite being total suckers for cultural fads, media hype, instant gratification, and any promise of ease.)

After Michel, Sedonia, and I had been in discussion for about an hour, Sedonia hesitated, then said, "But I have a deep conflict...." She paused a moment. An open person, she could readily confide, but hesitated now as though this conflict perhaps shouldn't be disclosed...or must be conveyed delicately.

"...I believe in God," she began, her eyes supporting the statement, "deeply. I have total faith in God..." she paused again, "but...sometimes it seems progressive not to be so poor."

I had hoped her conflict would be something I'd already worked on myself, and that I'd have at least compassion about or possibly some practical suggestion.

But I just looked at her and shook my head, "Sedonia, I have the exact same conflict."

We shook our heads together. How do you bet-
ter yourself and your life without leaving the less fortunate behind? How do you escape the 'hoarding' aspect
of bettering your life materially? If you believe in God,
how can you not share when people are suffering on all
sides?

"What does your husband think?" I asked after
another silence. (I liked this woman so much.)

"Look, he's a doctor and I'm a biologist. We
could make a lot of money in another country. A lot of
money.... But...only the rats abandon the boat. We're
not rats, we're humans."

This depth of soul emerged and re-emerged
from hidden springs in Nicaragua. When you least
expected it, there it would be again on somebody's lips.
"We are prepared to die," said Sedonia. "We'll fight
for this government. It has problems, like all governments, but it's so much better than what we had before.
Before, we had a tiny little 'hospital' up the road here.
And I remember women walking by with sick babies
and crying because they didn't have enough money to
pay the doctor. The doctor wouldn't see the baby if the
mother couldn't pay. Later I'd see the woman again
and ask about the baby and she would say the baby
died. Now we have a huge hospital. Everything's free
for everybody—medicine, anything they need. Now if
a doctor won't see a baby, we'll throw him in the sea."

"We will die if we have to," she went on, "to
show the world. We are dying already. A lot of soldiers.
All of us are ready to die. We're with the government.
It's been good to us, and we don't blame the govern-

ment for this war. The people are with the government."

"I write for newspapers in the United States," I told her then. "What do you think are the most important things to tell the American people about Nicaragua?"

"Tell them the truth. The truth."

After a moment, I asked, "Why don't the Nicaraguan papers mention the soldiers that die in actual combat? The ambushes and the road mines, those attacks are always in the paper with photos and everything, but there's never any mention of actual combat casualties from the battles."

"We have very few psychiatrists here," Sedonia answered. "The people would crack up if they heard everything that really happens in the war. It's bad enough what everybody knows and hears as it is."

As a bacteriologist, I wondered if Sedonia had any insights into rumors the local newspapers had mentioned about germ warfare.

She answered, "In 1981, '82, and '83, a bacteria appeared on our tobacco plants. A specialist—a plant pathologist from the U.S. who said he gets paid $500 a day at home—came here in solidarity and worked with us for free. He showed us how the disease affected the leaves of the plant and made them useless. We'd never seen this disease before. And we assumed it was delivered to us by some big, black, unfamiliar birds we'd seen—homing pigeon type of birds unknown to our region. We assumed they came from Honduras, then flew back there."

"Is it true that Dengue Fever is more widespread now?" I asked her then, questioning another rumor.

"Oh yes—everybody has it."

"Do the people think this is a result of germ warfare?"

"The people don't think that way. They just get sick and feel terrible. They don't associate it with the war."

"Do you?"

"Without a doubt. I'm a bacteriologist. I go into the lab, look at the virus, and see how contagious it is. It can easily be transmitted, or the germs let loose in, say, a school full of kids. Next day they've all got it."

Sedonia's eleven-year-old daughter approached the table then and they conversed in Spanish. As the girl walked away, I told Sedonia how pretty I thought she was. Sedonia watched the girl walking away, then looked back to me, "Do you really think so?"

"Oh yes," I said, "in a very special way."

"I don't teach her to be pretty," Sedonia said simply, watching her daughter across the room, "I teach her to be good."

~ *October 26, 1986, Bluefields*

We had the most miserable night of our lives sleeping in Sedonia's back room. The double bed was misleading; we thought it meant comfort (it's the only one we've had since our first night at the Santos). Sedonia brought in one of those mosquito coils you're supposed to burn all night in the room, but I explained (or tried to) that I always feel sick in the morning after breathing that smoke all night. But in Nicaragua, picky-ness is met with a shrug, "Fine, be fussy and suffer." (It's considered paranoia, not preventative health, to worry about sickness before you have it. Even the progressive Sandinista government is in the dark ages about natural health; doctors and medicine, both in short supply, are considered magical.) Anyway, we didn't light the mosquito coil, so our only recourse was to hide from the offenders inside our sleeping bags. It was about a hundred degrees in the room, so we were scratching, sweating, and swearing. Michel was practically suicidal. And whenever one of us managed to drift off for a couple of seconds, the other's thrashing would reawaken the sleeper. If there is a hell, it's probably a zen retreat compared to last night. And knowing we'd be exhausted for hitching in the scorching sun the next day was no solace.

The heat here, we've both concluded, is intolerable and removes any lingering inclination to live here. By the same token, just knowing we have the option to 'go home' separates us even more from this tragic reality....

Since we are at least smart enough to wear earplugs every night, wherever we end up sleeping, that morning we found ourselves in the midst of bustling family activity. We were in the spare room without a door that opened directly onto the kitchen, so everyone was milling around our bed looking for their t-shirt, getting the ironing board, munching on breakfast. Noting that the family was unfazed by us, and the mosquitoes were apparently satiated, we rolled over for forty more winks.

Sedonia heated up a fresh pot of beans for our breakfast, that she served the Nicaraguan way, topped with cream (made from powdered milk). We also had *hojada* (a tart, salty, white cheese), white bread, and sweet coffee with powdered milk.

Then, more than touched by Sedonia's hospitality, and inspired by her views, we had to say goodbye.

"Small house, big heart," she said again, as we left.

~ 21 ~

El Rama

With my invincible companion, I could tackle more than I ever could've solo, including this Bluefields junket—critical to my ever-morphing assessment of the truth around here.

As women, it comes with the territory that we're not always safe, and it's annoying being limited in how far we can extend ourselves. In a war zone, in a foreign country, or in any situation of compromise, mystery, uncertainty, or non-familiarity, it's SO advantageous not being an unattached female! Unaccustomed to having support, I felt beyond fortunate that Michel could accommodate my mounting sense of urgency. His helpfulness and camaraderie made everything more possible and more palatable.

Already roasting in the 10 o'clock sun, we marched toward the main road to flail our arms at traffic. Then, determining quickly that the few cars weren't going far, we trudged over to a bench in the shade. Hail Mary, it turned out to be a bus stop! Then, lo, a bus chugged in that was going all the way to El Rama!

Packed, of course, and we'd be standing, we still squirmed gleefully aboard.

Hell, Part Two.

Reaching Juigalpa yesterday, we thought we'd done the bulk of the road journey. Wrong-o. Now we had to stand (until we scored one seat) for five hours, pressed against everybody in a sweaty mass. And the pavement was a-shambles.

Because a bus on this same road had been ambushed two weeks earlier, there was legitimate fear of an attack or road mine today, so everyone, as one, paled at every bump in the road, and more so whenever the bus slowed down. When moving, a breeze through the open windows made it bearable, but we stopped often, sometimes as long as half an hour. At one of these stops, all the Nicaraguan men had to get off and show their papers. One man and his female companion were detained, and the bus continued on without them....

Next morning, at the Hotel Amy, we honeymooners woke at 5:30. The village of El Rama, nestled on the riverbank, was enshrouded in fog, collaged with muted blues and yellows of faded wooden houses and palm trees gray against the mist. Long canoes carved from hollowed-out tree trunks glided silently down the river. From the second story balcony of the Amy, half the town in motion could be viewed below—kids selling tortillas and unrecognizable fruits from bowls on their heads; funky shacks along the dirt lane offering cheese or vegetables out their windows; a little girl carrying a bucket of milk.

We scored some bitter coffee from a woman's stand across the road. Since she spoke some Creole (a brand of English), as the Caribbean influence is already apparent here, we learned that her father came from the Cayman Islands. She asked us if we liked this place.

"The river and the colors are beautiful," we said.

"Foreigners come here and say they like this place..." she mused, "but I don't think it's very good here." She looked around at the dilapidated state of everything, then back to us. "It's sad."

"Will you stay here?" I asked.

"I'll stay right here. It's my home. It's sad though."

"Is it very different now?"

"Yes. We can't get anything. No meat. No eggs. They don't send us anything. No sugar. No vegetables."

"Everything comes here from Managua?"

"Yes, when they send us stuff. And then some of the people get it first and they're greedy."

"Can't you grow things here?"

"Not anymore. All the men are in the Army. Or some went with the Contra. And the Army won't let us go out in the bush to farm, not now."

"Is the war very near here?"

"Oh yes, them fighting all the time. All the time.... I cry sometimes...all the women cry. My sons are in the Army and carrying guns now. Other women, their sons have died."

"What do people want to happen with the war?" I asked.

She said nothing.

She knew I was American, and I wondered if that was why she said nothing. "For the Americans to stop?" I asked.

"Yes," she said.

"I don't understand why the men here join the Contra," I said. "For the money?"

"I don't understand it either," she said. "I read my bible every day. I believe in God. But the war goes on…. I don't understand it. But the bible says we're gonna have hard times and we have to be strong. So we try to be strong."

On a corner house, this graffiti is scrawled: *"Somos un pueblo pequeño, pero valiente y fuerte."* ("We are a small people, but valiant and strong.")

We liked Rama. Weird out of the way place. We were the only gringos there.

A Sandinista soldier plucked us out of the long waiting line for the boat that morning. (It was a three-hour queue to guarantee getting aboard, should the vessel ever arrive.) The soldier requested our *documentos*. This is the norm, everyone is checked all the time — sometimes *Nicas*, too, to make sure they're not the Contra moving through. But, needless to say, Americans are given the most scrutiny.

This man took our papers and disappeared into an office for about fifteen minutes. Returning, he pointed out that I didn't have my embarkation card in my passport. I realized I'd left it in Managua with my stack of residency requirements. "I'm applying for residency," I told him, thinking fast about how to pass without this essential item. "And they have my embarkation card at Immigration in Managua." An untruth to cover an honest oversight…anything to avoid getting back on that bus to Managua.

Michel cast me a supportive-spouse glance indicating he could accept being turned back if it came to that. A bad sign. He then inaugurated a homespun fabrication as to why I didn't have the card. But I'd discovered the Sandinistas see through the song-and-dance—they like straight talk. In quiet English I asked Michel to let me handle it, and he stepped back.

The soldier resumed scrutiny of my passport.

"I have this instead," I pointed meaningfully at my visa extension stamp, in no way a substitute for an embarkation card.

"Yes," he said, then peered at me. "You were in Honduras, also?"

Before leaving the States, I had secured a working visa for Honduras because I thought we'd be driving through Honduras in the camper. I figured hot-headed Honduras would be more agreeable if I had a 'working' rather than a 'tourist' visa. Here in Nicaragua, though, an American with a working visa for Honduras is a party-pooper bar none.

"No, I wasn't in Honduras," I answered. "I just got the Honduras visa in case I had to travel there for my work."

"What work?"

My first weeks in Nicaragua I always showed officials my press card along with my passport. But lately I'd been finding it simpler and arousing less suspicion to say I was a tourist and to keep my press pass in another pocket. But now I'd admitted to being down here for work. "I'm a writer," I said.

"May I see your press card?"

I showed him my valid Nicaraguan card, but knew I was getting in even hotter water now for being sneaky about being a writer. "I also have a working visa for Guatemala...see? In case I have to travel in other parts of Central America."

"But your permission paper to go to the East Coast says you're going as a tourist."

"Yes," I said. "I'm not working right now. Just taking a vacation to Corn Island."

He was silent. (As well he should be — not too many vacationers around here.) He studied my eyes for the truth.

"When I write," I told him, without moving my eyes from his, "I write the *truth* about Nicaragua. That's why I'm here.... I understand though why it's necessary to check us very carefully."

He didn't say anything for a moment. Then slowly, he folded my permission paper and gave it back to me. He handed me back my passport. "Okay," he said, and smiled.

"*No pasaran,*" I said.

"*No pasaran,*" he smiled back.

~ 22 ~

Bluefields

'The Express' left at noon. The fare, 17 cents.

This vessel had been attacked five times since January. We didn't feel safe on it but decided not to think too much about the Contra—fear wouldn't protect us. Offering some semblance of security, there were seven no-nonsense soldiers with rifles standing on top of the sixty-foot craft, but there were also bullet holes in the windows.

Petra, the German *brigadista* who'd taken this river trip, told me when she returned that she'd been asleep on the floor of the inside cabin and had awoken to the sound of gunfire and all the passengers hitting the deck around her. She'd sat up to see what was going on and a soldier had pushed her back down. No one had been hurt, but bullets were fired. The Express just kept moving.

This was a four-hour sail and visually idyllic. Throughout our time on the glassy, green-brown river, we passed grass huts surrounded by families—the children often swimming—and sleek, tree-trunk canoes sliding silently by or moored beside huts. Total tranquility. Incredibly remote. Amazing that these people were able to stay so isolated with the Contra not far off. We often saw soldiers though, in canoes or beside the homes.

At dusk we sighted Bluefields in the distance. We'd been told that, as in all the Central American countries, the East Coast culture and ethnicity are more Caribbean — English widely spoken, with a prevailing Creole influence. And where, to the west, Spanish/European ethnicities dominate, here the origins are predominantly Black and Native Indian.

"The town look like nothin' from here," said Anders, a seventeen-year-old English-speaking Bluefields boy I was sitting next to, "but it's beautiful when you get inside." Anders attends secondary school in Matagalpa. When I asked him if he'd have to join the Army soon, he said, "I'm already in the Army, the Army of the Lord. And I can't belong to two armies…. I'm going to school to learn to serve the people. I don't want to be a professional because professionals only serve themselves. I want to help the people. And when the Army want me, I will tell them that somebody have to take care of the towns, somebody have to prepare to serve the people. If all the men go in the Army, who gwine to stay and take care of the town? Or if all the men die, we got no future. I tell them, and I stay firm. The Lord stand by me and they don't touch me. I doing what is right for me. Other boys my age they want to play around, but I must do this right away—there's no extra time. I got no choice about it."

Anders then indicated for us the direction of a hotel. But moments after stepping ashore, we were adopted by a youth called Cleveland and his brother Howard. They spoke Spanish and English, and looked more Spanish than black. We were fortunate they

latched onto us because that first hotel and the next five
that Cleveland led us to were all booked up.

The problem tonight was that the electricity was
off in the entire town, and had been for three days. So
all was dark, with only lanterns everywhere. An in-
triguing masquerade ambiance permeated streets dancing with silhouettes. Voices everywhere lent excitement
to the darkness, like a masked occasion where no one
knows who's who. Low hanging wooden balconies and
candle-lit alcoves contained people finishing the day's
business or drinking a beer. Through it all, Michel and
I moved along with our backpacks and our two guides.

After treading all over town for over an hour,
the "El Dorado" hesitantly took us in — after we nearly
begged for a room, somehow overriding their insis-
tence that without electricity and water it wouldn't be
satisfactory. We hadn't even learned the Spanish word
for 'satisfactory' — completely irrelevant in Nicaragua.
And the El Dorado was, for us, just one more extreme.
True, a shower would've been welcome — we were
filthy from the heat and all-day river voyage — but a
bed was the only deal-breaker.

As it happened, we got three single beds. So we
used a few precious drops of my canteen water to rinse
our hands, then went out for a beer, and sodas for our
escorts.

In the town's center, a tavern glowed inside from
the lanterns (soda bottles with lit gasoline-soaked rags
stuffed down the necks). At the fifteen tables within,
sat locals chowing down and guzzling *cervezas*. We
found a shadowy table in the midst of what looked

like a Hollywood set. Voices surrounded us and more passed outside the broad, open windows, all in a swirling blend—mysterious to newcomers who'd never seen the place by day. "If you made a movie of this," I said to Michel, "everyone would think you'd totally exaggerated." But the town bustled along in the blackness, townsfolk seeming to have adjusted to it after three full days.

Sadly, by day Bluefields was an unadulterated junk heap of dwellings, boats, and crude markets, all under relentless rain.

At 6:30 a.m., in my poncho, I went down to the wharf to inquire about boats to Corn Island while Michel attempted to sleep in.

"There's one leaving in six days," I was told. And I could "continue to check in at the dock every morning at 6:00," but nothing else was scheduled.

I stopped for a black coffee on my way back and had a long chat with an aging sailor named Juan. Like everyone here, he speaks English. On Tuesday afternoon, he's off to Puerto Cabecas, farther north up the coast, in his 200-foot freight boat that also takes passengers. Though I'm attracted to the tropics of Corn Island, I'm more enticed by Puerto Cabecas because it's a) inaccessible by road now, and b) legally off limits to gringos because of the war (quite likely because of the trouble between the Miskitos there and the Sandinistas). So I asked Juan if we could go along on his boat and he said sure.

"Do we need any special permission?"
"No."

He also said he'd be sailing back to Bluefields in five days.

I figured even if we got busted for being in Puerto Cabecas, the worst thing that could happen would be a stint in Sandinista prison — probably posh compared to our usual digs — and the best thing would be the FSLN flying us back to Managua and saving us a repeat of the bus-boat ordeal. We'd miss Corn Island, but, pertaining to the war, I've never once heard Corn Island mentioned.

~ *October 27, 1986, Bluefields*

~ 23 ~

Quien Sabe?

The sun's bright today, the sky a rich blue. And most of the houses and buildings in Bluefields are also painted blue. As for the 'fields,' *quien sabe*?

Saw another gringo this morning—tall blond guy with a camera.

Am having coffee this morning in a funky dive near the wharf. A poor choice for journaling, because some 'event' is about to take place practically in my lap. Two huge cans, the size of garbage cans, have just been delivered to the front entrance here and are being poked open by seven adults and four children with wrenches and screwdrivers. A hose is being connected and crates being placed to catch the fluid—whatever it may be.

Moments later the fluid proves to be gasoline, or possibly kerosene, and the fumes overwhelm me as people arrive from up and down the street, carrying containers of assorted dimensions, and line up to score their rations.

Two things come to mind again and again in Nicaragua. One is that this country at this moment cannot be judged, summed up, or even understood without knowing much, much more about the past—recent and distant. As if there's an odd sound, you want to know what it's emanating from. Whatever it is, it's weird and unsettling, and…not finished. Nothing is at rest here. But much of the strangeness is the inevitability of more trials to come; Nicaragua's effort still hangs in the balance. For all the suffering, no one would say the worst is over. But to touch down in the middle of it and try to really comprehend or define it seems…shallow.

Yet, there's magnificense in outsiders coming here and caring as much as they do. That compassion and support is measurable and touching, And it offers subtle and inexplicable reassurance, felt nationwide.

A recurring impulse is to try make something out of this whole delicate paradigm. Art perhaps…. But beauty is covert here. I think of artist friends back home and wonder how they would translate this. All I've personally come up with—aside from describing it all daily with words—is an urge to photograph the faces in black and white…. But when I try to, I either get just snapshots or self-consciousness. There is intense, though sporadic, beauty here, in the juxtaposition of incredible hardness—sacrifice, strength, and survival—and incredible softness—vulnerability, pain, openness, and *hope*.

Nicaraguans are a proud people. And, misunderstood or out of context, pride may seem not pretty. But the painful pride here of overcoming obstacle after obstacle is a kind of treasure. If these people make it, they'll be a rare breed. And, just glancing at the faces, an American might see Latino people like those in shopping centers in any Los Angeles suburb. But there's something more in the way they do things—patience and persistence, toleration for petty hassles, and a 'togetherness'—that we independent Americans love to think we've risen above. It's called *solidaridad* (solidarity), a word used constantly in Nicaragua, that has gut-wrenching meaning. We don't just 'care,' we don't just 'sympathize,' we're IN IT. And we're in it together.

The boat to Corn Island doesn't leave for six days. This morning I learned there's also a daily flight, but it's booked up for the next six days, meaning if we don't sail on Juan's boat, Bluefields is our home all week.

The only side trip to take in Bluefields is a short hop by boat to "The Bluff," an islet across the bay. So, yesterday afternoon, after the rain stopped, Michel and I hopped a small launch and zipped across. I'd been warned by other travelers (not lately, since we've only seen that one other gringo since leaving Managua) that The Bluff was underwhelming.

Said warnings proved accurate. But the captain of the skiff, Jim, had info about Contra activity in these parts, making it worthwhile for me. With his lovely face and laid-back manner, in keeping with the Caribbean influence, Jim also spoke English. I asked if he knew anything about the attacks on The Express, the boat we'd ridden from El Rama.

He nodded. "The Express has been seriously attacked twice. In the second attack, about three months ago, a woman passenger was killed. A bullet popped her brains out. There was another boat, you know, before The Express, but the Contra burned that one. They stopped it and then they burned it. Yeah, that first boat would stop for them, but not The Express. The Express keeps going no matter what, because they burned the first one...."

"How did they stop the first boat?"

"Well, they were in another boat and they ordered the passenger boat to pull over to the shore. The captain did what they said because he thought maybe then they wouldn't hurt the passengers. Then the Contra made everybody get off. All the passengers did what they were ordered to, but there were five soldiers on board who wouldn't get off. The Contra told them they were going to burn the boat anyway. And the passengers tried to get the soldiers to get off, but they wouldn't. And the soldiers burned with the boat."

"They wouldn't get off and they burned with the boat??"

"That's right. They're guerrillas."

Jim then mentioned that he, too, is on that river a lot, in his own boat.

"Isn't it dangerous?"

"No, they don't bother us. As long as we don't carry soldiers on board."

"Really?"

"Yeah. See that green boat over there? The Contra stopped that boat up on the river a while back, and they checked to see if any soldiers were on board and there weren't. And they told that captain that if any of us carry soldiers, then they'll get us—otherwise, no."

"But then how can the soldiers travel on the river?"

"They have their own boats. They have theirs and we have ours."

"Is Bluefields generally pretty safe?"

"Yeah. Not much trouble. There was an attack up here about a year ago."

"They attacked the town?"

"Twenty-three of them attacked the Army base up here," Jim pointed to a nearby Army station we'd walked past earlier in the day. "But they were all killed."

"All twenty-three of them?"

"Yeah. The Contra came by boat around 5:00 in the morning and attacked that base, but they all were killed."

"Any Sandinistas die?"

"Two. Then they laid out the twenty-three Contra bodies in the park up here so everybody could see who they were."

"Were any of them recognized?"

"I think a couple were from here."

"Why do they join the Contra?"

"No one really knows."

"For the money?"

"Who knows?"

~ October 28, 1986, Bluefields

Part Nine – Bordering on Chaos

~ 24 ~

Hotel Dipp

Bluefields is not the kind of place to spend more than a day. We're going on four now and rapidly losing our marbles.

After seeing the serious military installment at The Bluff, and being told more than once that every boat that passes through there is inspected, and that no gringos are allowed to go to Puerto Cabecas, we decided not to sail on Juan's freighter. Though we might get away with it—*and I was so keen to go*—it's just not fair to side-step Sandinista security measures and complicate their situation further. It's even cavalier, and possibly foolhardy.

Ergo, yesterday morning, after our daily 6:00 a.m. perusal of the wharf, to ensure no water craft was sneaking off to the island without us (as one did the previous morning), we went out to the Bluefields airport to see if anything was flying out.

At the air strip, there was a wooden passenger shed of sorts, blue of course, and ample by shed standards. Inside was an affable, elderly, black gent in a cap who advised us to stick around and see what came through. He said for twenty dollars we could probably get a pilot to fly us to the island. However, there wasn't a plane or even another soul as far as the eye could see.

A while later, a six-seater touched down from Managua for an hour, then headed out from whenst it had cometh. The rest of the day was uneventful, aside from some tasty rice and beans we scored from a *rancho* atop the hill. Yet all day we were encouraged to wait. "A plane's coming that will go to Corn Island," said two or three strangers pretending to know. At 3:00, after naps and…not a bad day really, we hopped the bus back to town with all our belongings. The return was slow because most of the way a funeral procession on foot preceded our bus.

The local papers today expressed alarm about American preparations for attacking Nicaragua. One article mentioned "500 U.S. Marines training just inside the Honduran border to Nicaragua's north," and America speaking of breaking diplomatic relations with Nicaragua (right before the U.S. Congressional elections, precisely when Nicaragua predicted this would occur). I was so disconcerted, I wrote an article myself called "Countdown," about how grim the immediate future appears from here.

But then there was this, [63] so who knows?

63) *"The Reagan administration has tentatively decided to train Nicaraguan Contra troops in the United States, after Costa Rica, El Salvador and Honduras objected to use of their territory," US officials said yesterday.*

The Army, Navy, Air Force and Marine Corps have been directed to make detailed recommendations for suitable training sites in the United States, sources said. They have been told the site must be remote to minimize adverse publicity and American citizen opposition.

— *The Washington Post, October 27, 1986*

Rereading my own article, I scared even myself, and told Michel we were being frivolous going to Corn Island. Plus, the boat isn't leaving till Friday. Not to mention legitimate concern about getting back from there.

So, now we had no plan at all.

Michel hated the "El Dorado," though I actually found it above average. (One star.) My bed wasn't uncomfortable and this was our first inn with no conversations in adjacent rooms. An unpleasant smell pervaded the premises, and there was no electricity or running water, but such would be the case everywhere since the town generator remained defunct. But, those trifles aside, it was altogether delightful. Still, Michel wanted to boogie.

After the airport, we scouted around, only to find four other hotels, no better than our current dump, all

full. However, at the no-star Hotel Dipp, we finally
talked a woman into admitting us. Persistence pays in
Nicaragua. Talking people into servicing you is part
of the learning curve.

Michel wasn't cheered by the sight of our new
nest. It had one chartreuse wall, two windows—both
without views and one without panes but vines in
it. There were two sad little bed frames, unequal in
size, with shabby three-inch mattresses, and a virtually non-functioning bathroom in total darkness.
The wood floor of our chamber had lots of suspicious
cracks, and we were soon to learn whose night clubs
they were.

We had now decided to go back to Managua
tomorrow, on the five a.m. boat upriver—the deck (no
pun intended) was stacked against us in Bluefields.
General danger, the power outage, and the dismal
town itself made it impossible to spend two more days
waiting for some phantom boat to Corn Island. So we
set my alarm for 4:30, murmured *buenos noches* across
the room, and stuffed in our earplugs. Using our
sleeping bags as bottom sheets, we wrapped ourselves
mummy-like in the single sheet on each bed to fend
off the mosquitoes. Aside from the loud motor of the
village's one auxiliary generator being used to light
the bingo game across the street, it was quiet enough.

About forty-five minutes later, some young
man with a loud tape player took up residence down
the hall and that was it for the sleep society. My exas-
perated mate was now stalking around in total frustration, eating oranges and smoking cigarettes on the

hall balcony. Two hours later, around midnight, the music stopped, he returned, and we again bid each other sweet dreams.

Moments later, the overhead fluorescent light sizzled on—electricity had returned! The plumbing came on, too, and as the toilet became the Trevi Fountain, shooting a jet-stream across the bathroom (there was no lid on the tank part), and leaking furiously out the bottom, we watched a few dozen giant water-bugs evacuate our luggage—open on the floor since the chamber had no furniture—and flee terrorized back into the floor cracks.

In a frenzy, we grabbed our scattered accoutrements, shook them, shoved them back into our packs, then zipped everything up. Michel snatched a small plastic bag of powdered milk (my attempt at *leche* for morning coffee) off the floor and it spilled all over because the roaches, bless their hearts, had bitten holes in the bag. We'd just bought it though, after searching for powdered milk for several weeks, so we shoved the remainder of the bagful into another plastic bag—all the while overly aware of the bathroom crisis. We swept the mess on the floor out the door with a folded newspaper, then naked Michel took gaffer's tape (a favorite carry-along of his) and taped the plastic bag of powdered milk to an upper portion of wall. Still giggling at the degree of weirdness we'd arrived at, I said, "That's gonna fall down."

Michel's unshakable faith in the tape trumped my pessimism, and he spun to the next task. The bathroom floor, built about two inches below the bedroom, was filling with water, threatening to flood our entire 'suite.' There wasn't much point in troubling the arthritic proprietress over this littleness, but I couldn't envision any other solution to this toilet-gone-rogue. Michel, however, leapt into action, asking me to bring a flashlight over to where his bare derrière glowed silver-gray between the chartreuse wall and cruel fluorescents. With a stream of light on the subject, he now pulled a handful of machinery from deep inside the toilet tank. Then, as the water on the floor rose to high tide, he fidgeted with the rusty pieces. He pulled, twisted, and adjusted things, then delved back into the tank. Like the straight man of a comedy team, I held the flashlight.

In two seconds, Michel not only stopped the leak but brought the toilet to a state of perfection unknown in this country. What a guy. Then the powdered milk fell off the wall and spilled all over the floor again. As I swept the white dust out the door again with the folded newspaper, Michel began rigging the plastic bag to a wooden rod suspended across the top of the bathroom doorway. He affixed the bag with his tape, and it held just fine, but the rod gave out so the bag of powder hit the floor a third time.

At this point we completely resigned.

Four hours later, with little remorse, we left the Hotel Dipp by way of a front door that was locked by a small wooden chair placed against it.

~ 25 ~

Boat Schedules

Thumping along the unlit streets toward the wharf, we passed the many Bluefields residents who are well into their day at 5:02. "They're looking at us like we missed the boat," I said uneasily to Michel. So we asked the next person we passed.

"Ya se fue," answered the man. ("It already left.")

In submission, we relaxed our gait, but decided to get a second opinion. (We were learning.) "It didn't leave yet," this next person responded, so we again picked up the pace. The wharf was in sight now, at 5:04, but all too quiet. As we got to the end, there was no 'Express' to be seen, not even sailing off in the distance.

"Ya se fue?" we asked a few idle gentlemen, probably on their lunch break.

"It left at four," they answered.

"Four??"

"Yeah, it always leaves at four," they lied. (I'd seen it leave at five the day before.)

We also were informed, later that day, that you have to buy tickets for this liner the day before. So, even if we'd been there at four, we wouldn't have been granted passage.

Down to Plan Y or even Z now, we spent a few hours asking about boats to Corn Island again. One was scheduled to leave Friday, it seemed. As today was Wednesday, we voted to give Paradise one last chance, but we'd make triply sure we had TICKETS.

At the ticket office, however, the woman announced this week's boat was canceled. The next one would be a week from Friday. "Maybe." We rephrased the question a few times, thinking we were misunderstanding the Spanish, our luck couldn't be this shabby. And the poor woman got so fed up with us she was rolling her eyes as she spoke. Probably to get us out the door, she then suggested the *"Oficina de Impesca"* (Office of Live Fish), where we should ask about fishing boats.

We went there and were told no fishing boats were going to Corn Island. We persisted and were then told there might be an ice boat coming over, "Come back tomorrow."

"Why would they be bringing ice here from Corn Island?" I asked Michel, as we shuffled off, wondering how to spend our day.

"They're probably coming here to get ice," he answered. Though transporting ice for seven tropical hours in any direction seemed bizarre.

We opted now to bus back to the airport and try our luck there for Corn Island, Managua, Fargo, Cairo, *anywhere other than Bluefields*. At the airport we were told there was a gasoline problem in Managua and no small planes were flying, just military and international flights. "It could change at any time though."

Since it was only 9:30, we lingered a while. We had no
hotel anyway, and there were eighteen or twenty other
hopefuls twiddling their thumbs on the four long bench-
es under the overhang.

After an hour or so, we climbed up to the control
tower, basically a tree house. "Nothing coming yet," the
controllers told us.

"Then why's everybody waiting around?"

"Maybe a military plane will come in," they said.

"Yes?"

"Maybe. Maybe one will come to pick up Commandante Campbell. He's here and he wants to go to
Managua."

"Will the military plane take all these people?"

"No."

"Some of them?"

"No…. But you can talk to the *Commandante* when
he gets here. If he comes. He might say you can come.
He might give preferential treatment to foreigners. Go
and wait, and I'll notify you if Managua calls and says
the military plane is coming. And if you see the *Commandante* arrive, you talk to him."

We waited another two hours, had lunch in a
different *rancho* that was 'closed for no reason' yesterday. Then Michel, exhausted from the industrious night
and advanced level of absurdity, reached his limit and
insisted we return to town. So we checked back into the
El Dorado—not remotely comprehending why it was so
named. (Hotel Dipp totally nailed it.)

That evening we took our routine turn up the
wharf, querying about boats. Tonight the pier was

swarming with activity. Halfway to the end, we observed two huge Army trucks about to leave the dock.
Sauntering past, we saw that each was towing an anti-aircraft weapon. I'd heard, months ago, that the Sandinistas had finally acquired some of these, and was glad
to have it confirmed. As Michel moved on down the
quay, I hung back to ask the attendant soldier a question or two.

First I politely smiled and studied the amazing
weapon. (Imagine this in the United States, "Excuse me,
Lieutenant, I'm a foreigner and just want to scrutinize
your most valuable weapons, here on the public pier.")

"*Sovietica?*" I asked the calm, dark-eyed soldier,
who wasn't more than eighteen.

"*Si,*" he answered.

"*Funciona en la noche tambien, o solo en el dia?*" I
asked him then. ("Does it work in the night, too, or only
in the daytime?")

"*Todo el tiempo, todo el tiempo,*" he responded ("all
the time, all the time"), waving a hand across it. This
machinery was the Sandinista life-line. With this, there
was hope. Everything hinged on this.

Michel returned and we meandered to the
wharf's end where another huge truck was idling. A
giant barge had arrived, piled high with cargo, most of it
covered by massive tarpaulins. Aboard, fifteen soldiers
were moving another of these anti-aircraft weapons
toward a wooden gangplank, to wheel it down to the
truck. We stood twelve feet away, watching the soldiers
move the mighty machinery. Surrounding us, soldiers
were milling around or observing. The scene was both
reassuring and terrifying.

After about ten minutes, and somewhat to our relief—because though we looked as naive as we were, we could've been *anybody*, and I am, in fact, American—a clean-cut young officer stepped up to us and asked to see our *documentos*. We handed over our passports and East Coast permission papers. The soldier regarded everything and immediately noticed our permission papers hadn't been signed by Immigration. "When did you get here?" he asked.

"Saturday night," we answered.

"Five days ago? Why haven't you had your papers signed by the Immigration Office?"

"We didn't realize we were supposed to until today," we said truthfully. "And today we couldn't find the Immigration Office."

He looked at us skeptically, our loyalty seriously in question. The Immigration Office, unbeknownst to us, was only a block away from the El Dorado.

"We are in complete solidarity with the Sandinistas," I ventured.

He didn't react, but I felt better cutting to the chase.

"Come to the Immigration Office at 8:00 tomorrow morning," he said, then walked off, with our passports.

Oops, looked like we weren't going to be on the four o'clock boat to El Rama on Thursday either.

Thursday morning, after Immigration—that, fortunately, was a breeze—we befriended Steve from New Zealand (the gringo we'd seen, who also had been waiting all week for the boat) and a guy named Frederick from West Germany. We also ran into some Australian twins we'd met in Managua who said a friend of theirs had gone to Corn Island and was a week late getting back. The telecommunications office there was broken down, supposedly, and returning from Corn Island appeared to be even trickier than getting there....

Meanwhile, another Nicaraguan newspaper article revealed possible American intentions to establish a "provisional government" in Nicaragua, "most likely in Bluefields." (Good luck with that.)

So Steve, Frederick, Michel and I were in the same boat, literally, at 4:30 Friday morning, heading back to El Rama.

~ November 1, 1986, Managua

Part Ten —
Interfering with Internal Affairs

~ 26 ~

Back in Managua

Final days in Managua. I'm visualizing my big, clean bed in California, the colors of my rooms, and the comfort of sitting and working in direct sunshine again without getting fried. Can't wait to sweep my floors and scrub sinks and tiles, after all the filth for eight weeks now. Can't wait to stretch and exercise, run on the beach, and be where good health is cultivated.

One could never fault Nicaraguans for any of the country's shortcomings. The war gets all the blame. Seven years of hardship is an eternity. And, taken one at a time, these are fine people — they love and laugh and worry about money like the rest of us. But their cultural heritage has been so badly battered…. I'd so wanted to go to Puerto Cabecas to see the Indians; maybe Nicaragua's essence is still within those tribes. Over here in the western portion of the country, people are running hard and fast from their past — whatever it was. And they won't look back. Unlike in Guatemala, European countries, even Mexico, there seems no marked heritage Nicaraguans cling to, no identifiable link to their own specific culture or previous way of life — no folklore, regalia, dance, festivals, rituals, music, feasts, even religious displays. (I suspect Nicaragua's history is too tragic.)

In fact, inside the military is the only hint of 'fashion' here. The only ones with vanity, who strut about or toss their ponytails, are the soldiers, male and female. Because they're actually provided food and clothing, they're also more attractive and confident than civilians. You see second-hand military garments, too, on regular civilians nationwide. Apparently soldiers will 'lose' a piece of their uniform then ask for a government replacement, while brothers and sisters 'find' a new shirt or pair of boots. This is one of the only ways to obtain clothing. A cap, a pair of guerrilla pants, a belt, are coveted items. They're free, well made, considered stylish, symbolic of solidarity, and plain nice compared to what else is available (nothing).

Nicaragua's shocking at times. In its favor, though, and in stark contrast with the squalid latrines, the people themselves are immaculate, even obsessive about cleanliness and the washing and ironing of clothes. From coast to coast, border to border, there's not a foul-smelling passenger on a bus, no one without shiny, clean hair and creased trousers. Even at the door of their shacks, the women and little girls appear in crisp, pressed dresses. Those you don't want to stand next to on the bus are the road-weary foreigners from North America and Europe.

Nicaragua Story

I generally get my writing done in the mornings, leaving Michel to chat with the colorful cast at the hostel, read the news, research whatever we're trying to find out, or just reshuffle our freight. I head out early to tackle the local newspaper cover to cover over Nicaraguan coffee. Following the news of the war is always my first daily task, still leaning hard on my Spanish dictionary. Today I'm in my choice spot, the only place this side of town to get breakfast and coffee before 9:00. (There was another place but it was closed down because the woman proprietor was caught buying dollars at a high price.) The three children here are my little buddies, and their whole extended gang is sweet and lovable with a strong, handsome grandma as ring-leader.

Then a glossy-haired, pony-tailed, tight-pants-wearing, female soldier with a briefcase under her arm, rolls up in her bright blue LADA (inexpensive Russian car that military and government workers—who don't have Jeeps—drive around in). This official takes the grandmother away, leaving other family grown-ups to discuss the flash occurrence, that I hope is something routine. I know these people don't buy dollars, so it's not that.

Soon enough, the LADA returns to the curb. Soldier and Granny both get out and go back into the house-cum-restaurant, Granny now carrying a bucket of eggs.

Sitting on this porch sipping coffee today, while Michel went off to explore the produce market on the far edge of town, I got enticed into a conversation, mainly because the initiator was a Greek—a pet nationality of mine and rare in these parts. Stavros is thirty-two, and has been in Angola, Iraq, Chile, two years as a political prisoner in Greece, and is now two months into his second stint in Nicaragua. We ended up spending the whole day together, getting my errands done while chatting about how to make these poignant Nicaragua weeks and months into something useful to the world….

Stavros explained that he's a member of the non-Soviet Communist Party of Europe and has come to Nicaragua for one year as a representative of that group. The Sandinistas have approved free residence for him at the elite "Cultural Center." But two days ago, a uniformed man knocked on his door and said, "You are being asked to leave. Please give me the key to your room and leave the hotel right away. You are being given fifteen days to leave the country."

Stavros suspects he "talked too much," and thinks he might have questioned things to the wrong person. Monday he's going to the office of Commandante Nuñez to find out why he's being asked to leave. Offended, he's hoping for a decent explanation. But after spending the day with him, I noticed more than a smattering of sass in his remarks about Nicaragua and how things are done here.

~ *November 5, 1986, Managua*

~ 27 ~

Heating Up

I'm sitting by the pool at the Intercontinental, one of the more serene pastimes in Managua, if not the whole country. It's pleasant having trees around instead of houses pressing in with the layered cacophony of twenty-member families. Not to sound spoiled, but writing does require a degree of tranquility.

Yesterday, I again ran into John, our Fulbright friend, who now says Embassy security has clamped down on him. He's no longer let into the Embassy as freely and they're withholding his government ID card that makes everything easy. Living at the Chipito, he says, has hinted to Embassy associates that he may be leaning slightly left. He said one staffer at the Embassy chided to another, "John lives in a *barrio* several blocks from the Embassy, don't you, John?" He sneered the word *'barrio,'* not knowing that it simply means 'neighborhood' in Spanish, (not 'funky neighborhood,' as it usually means Stateside). But, to keep his ear to the track, John needs to spend time with us, the ones researching this war on the ground, not those taking orders from Washington. Plus he's young and they're all much older.

But, before it became a hostel, the Chipito was a 'love hotel.' That's why each room has its own door to the street. "Before we had a house," a cab driver confided to me, "my wife and I used to go there and make love." And the love hotel is hardly on a par with Embassy residences, all endowed with guards, maids, cooks, fire alarms, and cars. (That opulent, Embassy-adjacent neighborhood is also home to the mainstream journalists.) Another betraying behavior of John's, he suspects, is that he doesn't chime in appropriately during Embassy conversations. Thus...his ID is tardy in coming.

Last Saturday he popped into the Casa Grande, the Embassy country club, to find an important meeting in session to which every Embassy affiliate had been summoned except himself. At the meeting, they'd all been given a twelve-page, typed hand-out detailing 'evacuation procedures.' John entered quietly, sat in the back, and listened as emergency measures pertaining to 'an evacuation of the Embassy' were laid out. At the end, he was able to nab a copy of the hand-out that had fallen on the floor.

He now passed it to me, to promptly devour front to back. We agreed its design is purposefully non-specific, making more mention of fires and earthquakes than war-related emergencies, and not even naming an American invasion (that they'd probably call an "emergency safety initiative" or a "protective measure thwarting a Nicaraguan invasion of the US"). But the full Embassy staff had been instructed to study this memo and make all advance preparations outlined in it. John said there was a lot of nail-biting in the room. According to this paper, all Embassy associates possess walkie-talkies with which to communicate during said "emergency." In other words, no one but the group itself (even John doesn't have a radio) will know about the evacuation until far more obvious signals are in effect.

The Nicaraguan paper today said, "The presidents of El Salvador and Costa Rica have been invited to Washington in the end of November." Both countries border Nicaragua, both are heavily backed by the U.S. (though Salvador is in a civil war over it). The paper also said that, according to Elliott Abrams, the Assistant Secretary of State for Human Rights and Humanitarian Affairs under President Reagan, the purpose of these countries meeting in Washington is "to exchange opinions on the regional crisis *in the critical moments.*" [64]

> *64) Elliott Abrams played a crucial role in propping up dictators in El Salvador and Guatemala, as well as the Contra death squads in Nicaragua—all in the interest of staving off left-wing movements (and presumed Soviet influence) in those countries.*
>
> *He clashed regularly with church groups and human rights organizations, who accused him of covering up atrocities committed by the military forces of U.S.-backed governments in El Salvador, Honduras, Guatemala, and the rebel Contras in Nicaragua. But Abrams accused all critics of Reagan's foreign policy towards Latin America of being "unAmerican" and "unpatriotic."*
>
> *Elliott Abrams is best known for his involvement in the Iran-Contra scandal during the Rea-*

*gan Administration, then entering a plea agree-
ment—pleading guilty to two misdemeanor counts
of unlawfully withholding information from Congress—for which he was convicted in 1991 and
sentenced to a $50 fine, two-year probation, and
one hundred hours of community service. But in
December 1992, he was pardoned by President
George H. W. Bush.*

— Wikipedia (and a source called 'Splinter')

Meanwhile, the situation on the Honduran
border is hot. According to President Daniel Ortega,
there has been recent, continuous, round-the-clock
fighting up there for days. A battle started October
24th and ended two days ago with the Contra finally
driven back into Honduras. The Sandinistas say two
hundred Contra were killed or wounded, twenty-one
Sandinistas died and sixteen were wounded. But this
is just the kind of event Reagan's gang could twist into
a "Sandinista invasion" of Honduras, the exact excuse
the U.S. might come up with when invading Nicaragua: "The Sandinistas provoked it. They threatened
Honduras up by the border."

It's a terrible moment in Nicaraguan history.

✖

Election Day in the United States. Forty percent turn-out expected "because it's not a presidential

election and there are *no big issues at stake* this time," said the American Air Force radio station this morning.

Michel and I are old hat at the Chipito now. A few weeks back, I avoided the multi-lingual chit-chat in the courtyard as I was busy writing. But, with the bulk of my work completed, I now sometimes spend hours in quality conversation, interrupted or joined by whoever passes to or from the shower. If you're not learning something, you can share your own stories and findings with newcomers. There are no tables or chairs in the cement courtyard, so we sit on a stoop with our backs against the wall on whichever side is shady.

Wayfarers of every nationality pass through, from Peru moving north — an accomplished band of flute players here at the moment — or Europeans and Americans who've been in Guatemala and are continuing south. There's one New Yorker who's been living in Managua two years, has residency, and works at the post office, wearing the same uniform as the Nicaraguans. There's Warwick, a journalist from Australia who's also been here over a year, and a host of others.

Yesterday, Steve (the Australian we met in Bluefields) and I were trying to get to the market to meet Michel, who'd gone there earlier. Two buses passed our bus stop for no reason, along with a bunch of empty cabs. So, after a futile half hour, I talked Steve into hitching. Recently arrived from Guatemala, he's not yet baptized in Nicaraguan transit.

The second car to come along stopped and an elderly gentleman welcomed us, in Nicaraguan English.

As we climbed in, a woman and her five-year-old boy asked if he'd take them, too. They were going to the bus station right next to our destination, so the driver readily agreed.

This guy, Miguel, was sixty-seven, had lived in Managua all his life, and had seven children between twenty-three and thirty-five. Two of them live in the U.S., two others are Sandinistas. Miguel was eager to talk to us, wanted to know about our observations here, and wanted to share his feelings. The first thing he told us was, "I was completely with the revolution in the beginning. It was fantastic. It was inspiring and good. Everybody really thought that things were going to get better for Nicaragua.... But now...now I don't know. It's not good now. A lot has changed."

We all agreed that the whole mess is beyond complicated. Miguel said he'd like to talk with us more so we made a rendezvous to meet at 5:30 for coffee, since we were approaching our stop at the market. Meanwhile, I asked the Nicaraguan lady, sitting in front with her son on her lap, how she felt about the war.

With almost no expression on her beautiful thirty-year-old face, she said that she'd just been told that her son was killed in battle, and she was catching a bus up to Matagalpa to find out if it was true. She said she believed it was true.

~ November 6, 1986, Managua

~ 28 ~

Zona Militar

Yesterday I cajoled Michel into walking to Tel-Cor (the post office) with me—a steamy, tedious trek undertaken only under pressing need. But I wanted to check out the preparations and rehearsals for the gala celebration coming up November 8th, the twenty-fifth anniversary of the death of Carlos Fonseca. [65] Telcor is down by Lake Managua and near the *Palacio Nacional* (formerly the National Palace, now an administration building), where the military parade and ceremonies will take place.

> 65) *Carlos Fonseca helped found the Sandinista movement. He was killed fighting Nicaraguan National Guard forces loyal to Anastasio Somoza.*

Nearing the area, we came upon a vast military encampment with hundreds of tents. For obvious reasons, some things—such as this monumental display—are off limits to the wandering foreigner. Despite guards positioned here and there, I took a quick photo anyway. Then, proceeding around the encampment and toward the lake, I snapped another shot from the other side. Risky.

In no time, three officers encircled me, wanting to know who I was and why I was taking pictures. Didn't I know this is a *zona militar* and photography is prohibited?

I told them I was here in solidarity and that I write, but had finished my work (true). I was simply walking to TelCor, I explained, and just took some creative shots of the Army tents juxtaposed against the skeletal remains of an office building destroyed by the 1972 earthquake (true), offset by the big hill in the background bearing the stark white letters, 'FSLN.' They all turned toward the view in question, then back to me, paused a second, then one said, "*Documentos,*" and extended a palm.

I led the entourage across the dirt road to where Michel was sitting in the shade trying to evade the *interrogación*. By the time we reached Michel, though, another officer was interrogating *him*.

Our documents were in order, and the soldiers were amiable. "But we'll have to take the film," they said, "because we can't let you have pictures of the military zone."

I took out my camera and, pointing to the frame counter, showed them that I'd only taken five pictures so far on the roll. "This film's very expensive," I said with sad hesitation, "and I'll be losing thirty-one pictures if I take the roll out now…." Any kind of waste is unconscionable in Nicaragua. I then swiftly changed the subject while quietly putting away the camera.

"Will I be able to take pictures on the 8th? How do I obtain the necessary permission for that?"

They helpfully said the Press Office was handling authorization cards and I should go there. After that we all smiled and shook hands. "*No pasaran,*" I said, and thanked them sincerely, apologized, and promised I wouldn't shoot in a military zone again.

"*No pasaran,*" they said back.

From TelCor, we could witness the parade rehearsal—nearly a hundred monster tanks were churning through. Planes and helicopters flew over in formation, then, completing the spectacle, a mammoth infantry came stomping along. We weren't super close, but as the procession concluded, the foot soldiers convened nearby in the big square by the abandoned palace. This area wasn't a military zone and would be televised comprehensively on the 8th for the world to watch, so I wouldn't be breaking rules taking pictures over there. Plus, I'd no longer be in Nicaragua for the actual event, so this was my sole opportunity.

With ultra-tight security surrounding this rehearsal, though, I was nervous about being stopped again. Glancing around for patrolling officers, and seeing none, I left my bag with Michel, who preferred the shade, and scurried over to the square. The foot soldiers had now climbed into the backs of open trucks and were waiting to be moved out. Standing behind a chest-high stone wall, I snapped a few quick frames then set the camera on the wall.

"Wendy!" a voice called out behind me.

I spun to my left to see Stavros the Greek waving and bouncing my way. I had wanted to see him again to hear what happened when he questioned his invitation to leave the country, so I waved back.

At that same moment, someone tapped my right shoulder. "*Migración,*" said a male voice. I pivoted right to face another uniformed Sandinista.

Meanwhile, the trucks were loaded and ready to leave…with my naked camera, sitting on the ledge, aimed directly at them.

"*Señor,*" I began with a trace of urgency, "is photography prohibited here in the public square?"

"No," he answered pleasantly. "*Documentos, por favor.*"

"Show him your passport," Stavros said authoritatively, arriving breathlessly at my side, as if to the rescue. Stavros was, actually, the one person I didn't need right now, having been formally evicted from the country for having a big mouth.

"My papers are with my husband," I explained quickly to the officer, "over there at TelCor." I pointed, then glanced longingly back toward the soldiers in the trucks — still there, but not for long.

"Don't be so nervous," Stavros interrupted, as if we were both guilty of something, then in paltry Spanish began to plead my case to the immigration officer.

I didn't need a spokesperson, lastly him. "Stavros, be quiet," I said, then turned back to the officer, who had a kind face. "*Señor,* will you wait here for me while I take just two photos of the soldiers? Because the trucks are leaving. Then I'll get the papers for you."

There was a short silence. "Okay," he smiled, and I rushed off with my camera.

Witnessing some thousand uniformed young
soldiers packed into trucks with their rifles was extraordinary in itself. They spotted me in a flash and grinned
for the camera, some raising their rifles. *

"*Por favor*," another male voice spoke behind
me. I lowered the camera to face two more officers.
One shook a finger at me to stop the photography, and
neither seemed pleased to meet me. "Photos are prohibited," said one, as the other said, "*Documentos*," and held
out a waiting hand.

The soldiers in the truck backed me with moans
of displeasure.

"This isn't a military zone," I explained to this
fresh inquisition. "Over there is the *zona militar* where
photography is prohibited." I pointed knowingly toward
the encampment. "But here it's okay. Another officer
told me... and he's already asked for my documents." I
turned toward where the other officer was waiting, only
to see him arriving at my side. My militia friends in the
trucks made louder disapproving sounds at the sight of
this third officer's approach. Looked like curtains for
the little *gringa*.

"I'm taking care of her," said this first officer to
this second batch.

"No problem," they nodded. And the first officer led me back to our hang-out under the trees, where
Stavros unfortunately was idling with yet another immigration officer (who'd materialized out of nowhere, as
they do). When I suggested we all stroll over to TelCor
for my passport (in Michel's keep), the officers said
they had to stay in the square. And clearly I wouldn't be

permitted to go by my lonesome because I might jump
a freighter to Tierra del Fuego.

"Can you go get her passport?" the first officer
asked Stavros.

"Sure," chirped Stavros, eager to participate,
and dashed off to TelCor in search of Michel, who
he'd never met. The two officers and I sat on a bench
under a tree and bird-watched as Stavros scampered
across the park. I was uneasy about any perceived link
to a convicted blabber-mouth, but didn't know how to
disassociate.

"Is he a friend of yours?" the kind-faced officer
queried.

"No!" I said too quickly, but was relieved he'd
asked. "I know him only a little."

"Oh," said the *señor*, standing up, "then maybe
it would be better for me to accompany you to TelCor
instead."

"Yes," I agreed, and we set off.

Arriving in front of TelCor moments later,
the officer, old chum at this point, watched me as I
scanned the area for the would-be husband. He didn't
seem to doubt my word, though there was no sign of
either Michel or Stavros.

Suddenly Michel appeared and, seeing my
escort, knew it must be *documentos* time again. As he
handed me my bag, I spotted Stavros heading towards
us at a trot. "There's Stavros," I muttered to Michel.
"Go head him off at the pass. He's the last thing we
need right now."

Michel managed to roadblock Stavros as the
soldier viewed my passport with reassurance, then

bid me a fond *adios*. Seconds later, Michel and Stavros cruised back. And, with the vicinity now clear of military personnel, Stavros could share what he'd researched about his own case.

He said, at Nuñez' office, they told him he'd been asked to leave because he "violated Article Four of the Constitution," specifically "interfering in the internal affairs of the government."

I suspected the charge was true.

* *That's the photo on the front book cover.*

Part Eleven – Leaving Them

~ 29 ~

Daniel

Making a stop at the Press Club on the way back to the Chipito, I got wind of a press event with 'Daniel' in ten minutes! Hardly dressed for the occasion, but at least equipped with my camera, I decided to cha-cha over there. Michel didn't have press credentials, so he continued on in the cab after dropping me at *Casa Gobierno* (Government House) where the Nicaraguan Press Office was located.

I expected the usual hassles—to be told I was too late, too early, too tall, or that I had to pay twenty U.S. dollars to update my underpants. And although they did relieve me permanently of my $25 press card because it had expired, they let me in. Since I looked like I'd been dragged there by a Roman chariot, I was relieved to find that the Hasenfus gang—the high-salaried, resident journalists, embedded CIA agents, and all the 'importance' they exude—were elsewhere. (Cocktail hour?)

About twenty-five *periodistas* (journalists), familiar faces and new ones, waited an hour in the lobby as all our bags and devices were methodically inspected in another room. Once our equipment was returned, an empty bus arrived and we filed on to be driven to an elegant convention center, built by the Somoza regime and now used by the Sandinistas for occasions like tonight's. Tomás Borge would be speaking to the original members of the *Frente* (the Front), the first supporters of the Revolution, those who either fought in the early years or offered their homes as shelter for guerrillas. [66] (Daniel would be there, but wouldn't be speaking.)

> 66) *Tomás Borge (August 13, 1930 - April 30, 2012), a renowned statesman, writer, and politician, was a co-founder of the Sandinista National Liberation Front (FSLN) and Interior Minister of Nicaragua under that administration of Daniel Ortega. He also held the titles of 'Vice-Secretary and President of the FSLN,' member of the Nicaraguan Parliament and National Congress, and Ambassador to Peru during his lengthy career. Considered a hardliner, he led the prolonged 'People's War' within the FSLN until his death. ***

* Pictures of him and Daniel, taken that day, may be found on my website.

The auditorium was packed with some two thousand *compañeros* (country folk, farmers) who had come in buses from outside Managua. Mostly between forty and sixty years of age, they were dressed up for the occasion. And when we, the press, arrived, they shouted their solidarity slogans that I'd heard so often, "*Aqui, alla, el Yanqui morira!*" ("Here, there, the Yankee will die!") For another hour, we all waited for the *commandantes* (government leaders) to take the stage.

I just wanted a close-up take of Ortega, to observe his manner and vibe. And eventually he, Borge, Nuñez, and three other officials, including two women I didn't recognize, entered and took places at a long panel desk up front.

A lengthy ceremony followed, during which various *compañeros* presented symbolic gifts to the leaders and made heartfelt speeches. Then, for the finale, Borge delivered an appreciated but endless oration.

Throughout the evening, I closely watched Daniel. He was alert and seemed cool, restrained, professional, keen, sensitive, emotional, and even ever-so-slightly sad. The moment he entered the intimate auditorium, he discreetly scanned everyone in the room. *Everyone.* In a slow, sweeping gaze, he took in the throng of loyal *Frente* members, then glided across the faces of the press contingent lined against one wall. Sensing no problem, he visually combed the other wall where we video and camera people were set up. This screening of the room, wall to wall, took only seconds, yet he missed no one.

Doing this, I could see 'Daniel' both reassured the audience and protected himself. I was taken by how openly he acknowledged each person, myself included. He then relaxed back into his *commandante* persona. But, because he wouldn't be speaking at this event, he was free to mentally drift off during the ninety-minute presentation, and seemingly did so.

After all the speeches, he and Borge came down into the crowd, where they both embraced, kissed, and spoke to all the women swarming them. Borge slipped away after a time, but Daniel alone stayed with the crowd, moving down the center aisle en masse with his loving supporters. And since this wasn't an actual press conference, but a sincere tribute to the *Frente* and *rare occasion* to be with their leader, security around Ortega was minimal. I was permitted to mingle and take pictures. And for the next fifteen minutes, I was two or three feet from the president as he inched through the crowd.

I was surprised and taken by Daniel's friendliness, his humility and accessibility, and his undeniable commitment to his people. Though I could never know the depth of what was being shared in that room, what the hugs really meant to them, it was a most personal reunion…of heroes really.

But then, wouldn't you know it, right in the middle of the best opportunity I'd had in Nicaragua, the Press Club bureaucrats herded all the *periodistas* back onto the bus. Probably the first time in the history of press that media left first when a head of state was milling around totally relaxed.

~ November 7, 1986, San Salvador, El Salvador

~ 30 ~

Michel

As I leave Central America, I definitely fear getting caught somewhere between total illusion and tragic reality (the U.S. and Nicaragua)....

The preparations for November 8th in Managua, the 25th anniversary, are like Liberty Weekend (1976) was to New York—gung-ho mania super-imposed on the city, and everyone sucked in by proximity.

The expansive center of Managua, basically the Intercontinental Hotel and the fields around it (where the earthquake and hurricane destroyed the former downtown), are off limits now to everybody but pedestrians and Army. You may walk through en route to someplace, but no vehicles other than military may enter. And, even if on foot, you're barred from the hotel, our convenient meet-up spot. A number of the actual hotel guests have even been relocated, to maximize security for the foreign dignitaries in town for the celebration.

Walking everywhere within a mile of the hotel or the palace means being constantly asked for documents. Of course I understand and respect it, but as an obvious target—no way can I blend in and escape interrogation—I don't love feeling like the enemy. If I hadn't had such an overdose of bureaucracy at the Press Office, I wouldn't mind, but…I've kind of had enough at this point.

Gate-crashing the rehearsal showed me this military extravaganza would be essentially an all-day pep rally under a mean sun. And I've never been enthralled by Sherman tanks. So, even though I had three more days on my visa, I decided to fly the coop. (Michel, returning to Montreal to rustle up some work, wouldn't be with me anyway.)

The airlines only allotted thirty seats per day for passengers leaving Managua, so my new LA flight might well be fully booked, but I figured some stalwart loyalist might postpone their ticket in order to attend the anniversary bash.

~ November 7, 1986. San Salvador

༂

Though Michel wanted as much as I to learn about and support Nicaragua, being somebody's wingman ain't easy. But I was the one with work pressures, searching for the real story, while becoming more and more confused and disillusioned.

Being blindsided at Managua Airport by Jacob Frances Warman seriously skewed my political orientation, and an unexpected urgency gripped me after that. Aware of the Miskito complexities, 'reporting the truth' was no longer straight-forward because I couldn't get close to the truth.

Michel remained in sync, but didn't have the wind in his face like I did. He could still inhale the tropics and enjoy lunch. But, even with his decent command of English, untranslatable moments arose when my frustrations (over the hassles, the suffering everywhere, even the burden of being American) exceeded his English. And I'd apologize, but couldn't muster translations. Would his linguistic acumen outpace my anxieties? Possibly.

But I became a bit driven. And I'd now also been apprised that *another* of the three editors I was writing articles for (this one at the *Village Voice* in NY) had been replaced, and my assignments there would not be honored. "Did you get the agreement in writing?" asked the smug editor-in-chief over the phone.

That precaution hadn't occurred to me (or them) in their Manhattan office last summer.

Well…their loss.

I was feeling off the mark about Nicaraguan issues now anyway; maybe just as well my assignments had vaporized. But so had the paychecks.

The Miskito ordeal was an element to the revolution previously unmentioned by *anyone* I'd ever spoken to from the U.S., Europe, or Nicaragua. (The footnoted info presented earlier in this book was unearthed decades later.) Back then—long before the internet—I

was alone in my need for answers and access to ob-
scure current events, that could only be understood by
spending time with and talking to the Miskitos themselves. There was *no one else* to connect with about it.
From my travels, it was obvious that—aside from the
Contras and Sandinista soldiers—no other journalists,
brigadistas, or *internationalistas* of any stripe that I'd had
contact with were even slightly aware of the Indian
dichotomy. With the exception of Petra and the several
gringos encountered in Rama and Bluefields, no one
we met ventured east of Matagalpa. And, of course, all
the mainstream reporters manufacturing propaganda
were the furthest possible cry from investigative. Only
inside the prohibited military zone, in the jungle, and
on the northeast coast, lay the answers. And I couldn't
go there.

But, once that classic Cowboys versus Indians
theme revealed itself, I started to feel sick inside. I'd
come down here psyched about where I stood and
what I needed to do, but was leaving feeling that old
scar tissue we Americans never seem to heal—first the
bullying of and lying to indigenous people, then the ul-
timate obliteration of their cultures, rights, dignity, and
autonomy.

And all the passionate, well-meaning leftists
worldwide, rushing to Nicaragua to aid 'the cause,'
didn't even know the Indians existed.... Everything
issuing from Managua and the Sandinistas, everything
offered on the world stage, had *nothing* to do with the
other side of this same country, a teeming jungle of
Indians.

To make matters worse, the Contra *did* recognize this massive divide and were exploiting it, against the Sandinistas. [67]

But there was no forum for this. And I even felt canceled out in a strange way.

67) —from 'Miskitos and Sandinistas,'
by L. Proyect, Columbia University
(no date given, but was long ago)

Many outside supporters of the Sandinista cause, including myself, had little understanding of the deeper Miskito struggle. All we knew was that there were some idealistic but inexperienced revolutionaries in Managua who had made some mistakes in places like Bluefields, on the East Coast. These mistakes enraged the Miskitos, who Ronald Reagan then manipulated into becoming Contras. But, unless we get past these clichés and begin to understand the true nature of Miskito concerns in 1980, we will never be able to understand one of the failures of the Sandinista Revolution.

The best presentation of the Miskito case comes from Charles R. Hale, an American anthropologist who was a Sandinista supporter. (He wrote the book, 'Resistance and Contradiction: Miskito Indians and the Nicaraguan State,

*1894-1987.') The more time he spent with Miski-
to people, the more he came to realize that the
government in Managua had misunderstood
their legitimate demands.*

*Hale explains that the same economic
forces that sparked the Sandinista revolution
against Somoza had also shaken up the Atlantic Coast. In partnership with Somoza, the U.N.
and the Alliance for Progress had also sponsored
large-scale Atlantic Coast projects the Miskitos
resented, including constructing a deep-water
port that interfered with their traditional fishing. The Miskitos faced challenges on all fronts.
But mostly, they felt left out of the economic
development that was taking place all around
them, none of which benefited them.*

∞✕∞

Back home, whatever scant updates people got
about Nicaragua were in abridged, watered-down
black and white. Two wildly polarized camps perceived
Nicaragua as either 1) our side — Sandinistas striving
for self-determination, with idealistic aspirations, and
wanting the U.S. to butt out; or 2) the other side —
communist encroachment into the Western Hemisphere via Nicaragua's socialist leanings, so the U.S.
has to snuff the Sandinistas (covertly, since the American public won't stomach another Vietnam). That
simple.

Nicaragua Story

Michel was contemplative about it all, but the pressures were mine. And, to this day, I'm not sure he grasped what was plaguing me as I became more rushed and more anxious to make the most of each day. But the sun was hot, buses packed, lodging ludicrous, and our hearts broken by everything around us.

Still…I was, and will always be beyond grateful to have had Michel share Nicaragua with me. He was the best partner.

~ 31 ~

Leaving Them

My new flight was at 8:00 a.m. The airline wanted passengers there at 6:00, especially standbys. But, consideirng cab-catching odds at that hour, I was lucky to arrive at 6:45.

Security at the airport was ridiculous; I've NEVER been checked like I was that day. My luggage was searched intensely three times before they even let me into the terminal, my passport as often. And by then it was well past 7:00, everyone having already boarded the plane, meaning I had become a special case attracting more attention. Just what I'd had enough of.

Michel had come along to send me off, but was relegated to bystander as I got processed like a raspberry being made into jam. By 7:30, I was cleared by the airline. But as I dragged my baggage to check-in, two soldiers in a doorway engaged in a knitted-brow deliberation as to whether to let me pass. They kept telling the airline man there was no serious problem, yet retained my passport, made phone calls, and wouldn't let me through. (That demon visa for Honduras probably the culprit.) The last minute, a phone call came in granting permission for me to board. I raced to the ticket counter, only to endure another intense search through my many pieces of cargo.

"It's been checked three times already," I said twice, feeling truly harassed, not to mention the unpleasantness of having men rifle through my personal effects. As a security man casually tossed my possessions like a salad, leaving the bags in disarray and nearly impossible to re-pack in the time given (none), I broke into tears. I hadn't realized how humiliating and belittling it is to be repeatedly interrogated, detained, and searched. You feel that your word, your appearance, and your credibility are all sorely lacking.

And I felt somehow betrayed, too…. I'd so passionately joined the Nicaraguan Revolution, given this segment of my life and livelihood to it, so supported its ideals and worked to spread the word in the U.S. Yet I was continually treated by government officials and military higher-ups like an enemy.

Of course there was no way they could know my position, what I'd written, or my true affiliations, and it was war time — I understood all that, but….

Well, I guess at the time I really *didn't* understand. What I wanted most was to just tightly hug them good-bye — I was leaving. Even going over enemy lines where there wasn't the slightest hint of war. *And they were all staying.*

It was so unfair. And so hard to leave them to their fate. I had options, they didn't. It was heartbreaking. I *loved* them….

With all my soul I just wished them the strength and peace they so needed and deserved. But they didn't know me or know these feelings….

Now I was too hurt to look any of them in the eye.

But…they were taken by my tears. At this point they'd finished searching the pack with the typewriter and xeroxes of all my previously published articles about Nicaragua. They motioned me over to the baggage and indicated I could close them up now. As I crammed things in haphazardly and fussed with the straining zippers of my luggage scattered all over the floor, I muttered audibly in Spanish, "I came here to write *good* things about the Sandinistas." The ticket lady sympathetically helped me inch the last zipper closed.

Then I stood up and looked at the men through the messy tears and embarrassment. "I'm not a terrorist," I said, pulled on my backpack, and walked back to where poor Michel (the one person who did know my intentions, and who'd be staying in Nicaragua a few more days) was barred from entry in the doorway.

It was a bad way to say goodbye. "Don't take it personally," he said, backing me to the last second, as we gave each other a hug that could never encompass all we'd gone through or all we meant to each other. Then I clumped off to the final immigration stop.

As I showed my passport one more time, hid my face, and brushed away tears that wouldn't seem to stop, one of the men who'd searched my baggage reappeared by my side looking very sorry. In the gentlest way, he apologized for the necessity of such security measures. I thanked him for comforting me, but was torn up just the same—about all my feelings about Nicaragua, about how bizarre everything had become here, even about how hard it is to love anyone in times of war because life itself gets so strained.

I hurried out to the plane, aware that I'd left in tears last time, too, but those were tears of wanting to stay. This time I was leaving three days early in tears of discouragement.

I got on the plane through a rear door and collapsed into an aisle seat in the last row.

Geez....

This was one revolution that was going to proceed without me.

That's when I noticed Elliott Abrams and his interpreter and bodyguard sitting quietly straight across the aisle from me — they, too, keeping a low profile in the rear of the plane.

Abrams recognized me from a press conference I'd attended and now said, "How're you doin'?" in his southern drawl.

As we glided down the runway, I instantly grasped why airport security had been so overblown. If anything happened to Elliott Abrams, the Sandinistas absolutely would be blamed.

Or...perhaps ol' Elliott had something up his sleeve and me and my demon visa, in the seat next to him, were part of his scheme....

No matter what, from a security guard's position, I did look a bit odd — Yankee trying to catch a flight without a reservation, arriving an hour late for a standby seat, leaving the country the day before the great celebration (not solidarity behavior), apparently wired in wicked Honduras, toting unwieldy amounts of cargo including tape recorders, electronic typewriter, cameras, extension cords, and battery rechargers…. And the only open seat was the one they'd intentionally kept empty, next to Elliott.

I would've checked me four times, too, with that dude on the flight. In fact, I would've kept me in the airport and let the plane fly. [68 & 69]

So I instantly forgave the Sandinistas. And I hope they forgave me for the many, many times I put my spoiled American impulses before the huge reality of their God-awful war. I was in solidarity though. And I disseminated the truth as best I could discern it.

More than anything else, the Sandinistas made me feel…lucky indeed.

And they made me feel.

68) *Abrams has continued working in high-ranking government posts under every administration. As of September 1, 2020, his current government position was 'The United States Special Representative for Iran and Venezuela.'*

— Wikipedia

69) *The failure to hold people accountable for Iran-Contra, one of the worst scandals in American history, has produced a society where Abrams is right back in power and Oliver North is running the NRA.*

And at the time of publishing this book, Elliott Abrams was recently questioned in Congress by Democratic Representative Joaquin Castro about involvement in recent weapons transfers to opposition groups in Venezuela.

— *from an on-line source called 'Splinter'*

~ End ~

Epilogue #1

I had one editor, George Wiley (at *The Easy Reader* in Hermosa Beach, California) who I adored working with (and who didn't get fired). He accepted every story I pitched, frequently making them cover stories, and used all the photos I routinely included. Most of all, he shared my point of view.

On my return, George ran the two stories he'd consigned me to write. And as I delivered the second one in person, he eagerly wanted to know what it had been like in Nicaragua.

I hesitated, not sure anymore how to answer that.

He watched my face and waited.

"Well—"

"Tell me."

I didn't know where to begin.

"What did you find out? What were your strongest impressions?"

"It's complex…" I faltered. "Hard to put into words— It's complicated down there…."

"What do you mean?"

I let out a sigh and my eyes began to water. George just watched and waited.

"My heart is broken," I said finally, with a deep sigh. "That's my overriding experience of Nicaragua."

"Why? What do you mean?"

"It's just…. It's just a mess. The children, the women, the hopelessness…."

"That's the story I want," said George, tapping my sternum. "Whatever it is you're feeling right now, that's the story I want. Write that. Write that and bring it to me."

Here's what I brought him:

In Nicaragua, Mobilization is *Todo*

There's a certain romance in revolution, especially for Americans who viewed the 1960s social revolution as incomplete. The Sandinista war cry of "We won't surrender or sell out" rings a forgotten bell for some Americans. "*No pasaran*," everyone says. ("They will not pass; they will not overtake us.")

The Sandinista war was the first one I ever understood—probably because I'd never been in a country the U.S. was fighting—and I wanted more of this understanding. In the U.S.-Nicaragua conflict, all the information seemed to be down there, not up here. In Nicaragua, there were stories in the air, history in the hills.

My second trip to Nicaragua though, afforded not the novelty of war but the reality of it. The soldiers weren't symbolic this time, but martyrs, guinea pigs in the experiment of self-determination. As weeks went by, Sandinista ideology meant less and less; the slogans came to be tired pep talks to an exhausted people. The 'meaning' of the revolution, all that had been fought for and won, from that moment that began with the toppling of Somoza in 1979, was becoming again an impossible dream.

Begun on the most optimistic note, this second visit was ultimately an experience that burns inside still like an ulcer. Because, in Nicaragua, a kind of household heroism is required of everyone. But when everyone's a hero, no one's a hero. The amount of bravery in Nicaragua and the absence of glory were jarring to an armchair veteran of U.S. TV wars.

I saw a boy of about five climbing a tree. He could only use one hand because the other held his shorts on. The elastic was gone. And needles, thread, and snaps are as hard to get in Nicaragua as money. In the next weeks, I saw more children holding their tattered pants on, and playing with only one hand.

Nicaragua could almost be called a children's country. A cluster of kids would be an apt emblem for the Nicaraguan flag. If you sit down for five minutes on a ledge or tree stump anywhere in the country, a ragged, brown-eyed swarm will soon surround you. The least shy will begin the questioning while the shyest stares wide-eyed and the rest clutch each other, giggle, and scrutinize you to the last mosquito bite.

These sidewalk sessions invariably end up with all the kids gingerly touching your notebook, your pen, the stripes on your socks. (Watches and rings of gold and silver produce such trance-like states in children and such longing in adults that you wish you'd left them home.) Jokes go farther with the children than perfect Spanish, but anything you say or do will make their day. And once they light up, they keep glowing.

Of the three and a half million people in Nicaragua, half of them are 14 years old or less. And so many

men are in the Army (70 percent) that the civilian population appears to be largely groups of children and their
mothers. The whole country's a kind of playground
with every grown-up instinctively looking out for the
children—anybody's. On buses (always packed), seated
adults automatically reach for the babies of the standing passengers. The longer you spend in Nicaragua, the
more involved you become with the children.

The kids pull their weight though. The girls help
their mothers in the mornings (the day starts at 5:30),
then go to school. At six or seven years of age, boys are
selling morning papers. Everybody old enough to make
change is a food vendor at bus stops, anyone old enough
to have a younger sibling is a babysitter. And children
pulling wooden carts or carrying loads on their heads
are part of the traffic everywhere.

The children know all about the war, and that it's
coming down to them. They reflect the various political
views of whoever's raising them (broken or fatherless
homes are numerous, from war-related deaths or pressures), but all the little boys expect to fight. At 16-and-
a-half or earlier for some, they join the war.

The innocence and strength of these little people
is as gripping as their black eyes and white smiles. It's
rare to see a Nicaraguan kid crying, and sad when you
do. To take a few home was a recurring temptation, as
was the urge to lie when they asked "What country are
you from?" Saying goodbye each time, and leaving them
to their fate, was a recurring heartbreak.

There was one skinny little guy begging in front
of the big Managua hotel that foreigners use as a meet-

ing place. His shiny eyes and puppy-like movements cut through all political thought about the war. He was about six. One arm was a stump, the other was in a cast. The money I gave him seemed an empty ritual that merely underscored the fact that I'd leave Nicaragua and he'd stay.

As I came out of the hotel an hour later, his fragile little frame and baggy clothes were asleep in the grass—his tragic limbs askew as if he'd blown over. As I tried to leave a bigger contribution in his open palm to surprise him when he woke up, his eyes opened. Without even registering what was happening, brightness filled his face and an automatic smile started across his lips.

Pro-Sandinista, anti-Sandinista, everybody is suffering. Death and sacrifice are the daily fare. Traveling on crammed buses (on which your body is twisted out of shape for hours at a time), foraging for food, sleeping in seedy hostels where bathroom doors don't necessarily close, disintegrate even an outsider's dignity. Toilet paper is as scarce as everything else.

Trudging along with heavy loads in the white liquid heat when buses and cabs are too full and too few, you learn the short-term tricks (like '*mañana*'), but long-term survival in Nicaragua, as it is now, is literally impossible.

The Sandinista government, too, endures a psychological torture. To protect the country from the Reagan-blessed Contras, incredible organization, strategy, and material are required, not to mention unbendable soul, stamina, and sense of purpose. But

protecting the country is a double-edged risk: if the
Sandinistas rest their defense for an eighth of a second
to attend to the other needs of the people, they fear the
U.S. will take over Nicaragua, creating whatever scenario is necessary to get the job done.

If the Sandinistas continue their full-tilt (and
seemingly effective) militarization, at the expense of
society, they stand to lose the love and loyalty of a people once world-renowned for their morale, now utterly
depleted.

Being in the Army can be something of a pathet-
ic solution to the food and clothing problems for some,
since most government resources are directed there.
But this isn't an option for mothers and children, or the
elderly, infirm or handicapped.

Humiliation is an awkward sensation, and a
tough pride the natural reflex to cover the awfulness of
it. Humiliation's undermining the Nicaraguan character. Rationing, shortages, hopelessness, and not being
able to progress as an individual or a family are debili-
tating the national psyche.

The non-military facets of the war, combined
with the terror of Contra attacks, as well as injury and
death from the battles, are squeezing Nicaragua dry.
And anyone familiar with the original Contra strategy
will recognize the fulfillment of its plan to push the
populace to a desperation that the Sandinistas can't
possibly relieve.

Once-familiar products—everything American—are gone with the U.S. embargo. The rebuilding

of international trade agreements takes energy, capital and years of diplomatic footwork, not easily affected while fighting a war.

This level of despair, which can only be called impending death, is not plainly visible in Nicaragua. One sees, instead, the tough pride. But the superhuman reserve that's required daily to accomplish even the smallest tasks—standing in lines for hours for white bread or a bus ride—reveals the hardship. The lack of complaint says more than complaining would. You learn an unimaginable patience there: gringos being always the first and only ones to roll their eyes in frustration.

No one mentions the Contra when riding the rural buses, for example. But if a stopped truck is passed on the roadside, all eyes rivet to the sight, everyone craning toward the windows, faces grave and jaws clenched, until it's ascertained that no road mine has exploded and no ambush has been (or is being) sprung.

The degree to which one can rise above hardship is the measure of survival in Nicaragua. Perseverance, humor and kindness are the last commodities available, valued as national treasures by those who have no others left.

— *Easy Reader, December 26, 1986,* &
The East Hampton Star, January 29, 1987

Epilogue #2 (Nicaragua Now)

70 & 71) — *from an article: 'The Mouse Kills the*
Cat: Augusto Cesar Sandino's Rebellion
against the US," by Daniel Kovalik
(website: 'The Internationlist 360,'
Feb. 21, 2022)

70) *It is now fashionable amongst dis-*
gruntled Sandinistas, the mainstream press in
and outside Nicaragua, and amongst even the
left in the US and Europe, to claim that the
current FSLN leadership, including President
Daniel Ortega, have abandoned Sandino's leg-
acy and the tenets of the Sandinista Revolution.
Even the dictator Somoza, shortly before being
gunned down (by Argentine revolutionaries in
1980) while exiled in Paraguay, put out a book
entitled, 'Nicaragua Betrayed.' It is not even
uncommon now to hear snippets that Ortega is
'the new Somoza.' *

* I myself saw that claim referenced in the infallible
Wikipedia. And, please, we give a banana peel about Anastasio Somoza's opinion of Daniel Ortega?

71) *According to S. Brian Willson—a Vietnam veteran turned peace activist, who lost his legs in 1987 protesting an arms shipment by train from the US to Central America, and who has lived many years in Nicaragua ever since—"the essential promises of Sandino and the Sandinistas to the Nicaraguan people have been fulfilled: 1) independence and sovereignty in the face of the US and its attempts to determine Nicaragua's destiny; and 2) land reform, education, and a decent life for the peasant population."*

According to the majority of Nicaraguans, Ortega and the Sandinistas have largely made good on both these promises. And that is why Ortega remains popular in Nicaragua (continually reelected president from 2007 to the present, 2022). They have given many hectares of land to the peasants; instituted free education and free health care; put money into affordable housing for the poor; electrified the entire country and built up the infrastructure; and significantly reduced poverty and extreme poverty. Nearly 100% of the food Nicaraguans eat is grown and raised by the peasants themselves. The Sandinistas have kept Nicaragua free of US interference, most notably by winning the brutal Contra War of the 1980s, a conflict that killed 30,000 and left the country and economy in ruin.

*I have been traveling to Nicaragua since
1987, and have watched a country with once
shocking levels of poverty become a prosperous
and developed society. If Augusto Sandino could
see his country today, I believe he would be proud.*

❧

In closing...for anyone wanting to portray Ortega
as the new Somoza, or a dictator, or for anyone believing
Daniel hasn't followed through on the Sandinista ideology, listed below are some of the changes Nicaragua has
experienced under his leadership.

Note that there was an interim government for
sixteen years when Ortega was not president (1990–
2006), and that government is known as 'the period of
neo-liberal rule.' And, briefly, here's why Ortega was
out of office during that interim.

> *72) from: 'The Contra War in Nicaragua'*
> *by Noam Chomsky, from the book,*
> *"What Uncle Sam Really Wants," 2002:*

> *The reason the Sandinistas lost the February
> 1990 election was because diplomatic fakery was
> used to crush them. An alleged 'peace plan,' con-
> cocted by the White House, Congress, Costa Rican
> president Oscar Arias and other Central American
> presidents, was made to sound like a good deal for
> Nicaragua. "If they moved their scheduled nation-
> al election forward a few months and allowed in-*

*ternational observation, as they had in 1984,
in exchange, the Contras would be immobi-
lized and the war brought to an end." So, the
Sandinistas held up their end, but Arias, the
White House, and Congress didn't honor
their side. Instead, the U.S. tripled CIA supply flights to the Contras. Within a couple of
months, the peace plan was totally dead.
(And Ortega was out of office.)*

But then Ortega and the Sandinistas were continually reelected, from 2007 to the present (2022). And... [73]

- *Throughout the second Sandinista period, the material
  and social position of women has again made giant steps
  forward. Because half of Nicaraguan families are headed
  by single mothers, infrastructure development promotes
  the liberation and well-being of women. This development includes the paving of roads, improving of housing, legalized land tenure, school meal programs, new
  clinics and hospitals, electrification, plumbing, literacy
  campaigns, potable water, aid programs to campesinos,
  and crime reduction programs.*
- *Nicaragua now produces nearly 90% of its own food,
  most from small and medium farmers, many of them
  women. 'Zero Hunger' furnishes pigs, a pregnant cow,
  chickens, plants, seeds, fertilizer, and building materials
  to rural women, given in the woman's name. The program has aided 275,000 poor families (over a million
  people).*
- *More than 445,000 women have received low-interest
  loans (0.5% annual interest).*

- Since 2007, 5900 cooperatives have formed, 300 being women's co-ops.
- Poverty has been reduced from 48% to 25%; extreme poverty from 17.5% to 7%.
- Since 2007, the Sandinista government has given out over 451,000 land titles across the nation, women making up 55% of the property owners.
- Potable drinking water has gone from 62% of the urban population to 92%; in rural areas, 28% to 55%.
- Homes connected to sewage disposal systems have gone from 30% to 57%.
- The percentage of the population with electricity has shot from 54% to 99%. Street lighting has more than doubled.
- Virtually everyone has a cell phone; free high-speed internet is often available in public parks.
- Nicaragua's road system is now amongst the best in Latin America and the Caribbean. More roads were built in the last 15 years than in the previous 200. Outlying towns are now connected to the national network.
- When the FSLN took office in 1979, illiteracy topped 56%. In 10 years, they reduced it to 12%. But in 2006, at the end of the 16-year neo-liberal period, illiteracy was back up to 23%. Today it's under 4%.
- The FSLN made education completely free, including a daily lunch of rice and beans to 1.5 million school and pre-school children. School children are given backpacks (and eyeglasses when needed).
- The country provides a free daycare system, currently numbering 265 centers.
- The medical system is free and vastly expanded. Chronic malnutrition in children age 6-12 has been cut by two thirds.

- *Nicaragua had the lowest number of Covid deaths per million of all the Americas. Schools and businesses never closed there during the pandemic.*
- *A new system of parks, playgrounds, and free recreation centers has been built.*
- *There are more than 1,700 healthcare units, one third built since 2007. The country has 77 hospitals, 21 new ones and 46 remodeled and modernized.*
- *There are now 178 'maternity homes' near medical centers for expectant mothers with high-risk pregnancies or from rural areas to stay during their last weeks of pregnancy. 67,222 women stayed at these centers in 2020. Maternal mortality has fallen from 115 deaths per 100,000 in 2006 to 36 per 100,000 in 2020.*
- *Nicaraguan mothers receive one month off work before their baby is born and two months afterwards. Men get five days off when their baby is born.*
- *Despite being a Catholic country, many places exist for women to get abortions. None has been closed or attacked, none is clandestine.*
- *Women make up 34.3% of the national police force. (NY and LA are 18% women, and Chicago is 23%.)*
- *Nicaragua has 102 'women's police stations,' where women can talk to female officers about crimes against them, receive counsel for trauma, and ensure violent crimes are prosecuted in a thorough, timely manner.*
- *The UN lists Nicaragua as the safest country in Central America, with a homicide rate of half the regional average, and half what it was in 2006.*
- *The Ministry of the Family conducts house-to-house visits to advocate prevention of both violence to women and sexual abuse of children.*

- 50% of public offices are filled by women, including cabinet positions and federal judges. It has the third highest percentage in the world (after Spain and Finland) for women in cabinet positions.

73) — from: "Why is the Nicaraguan Government Demonized by both Liberals and Conservatives when Nicaragua has seen Great Progress under the Sandinistas?"
— by Stansfield Smith, March 28, 2022
(from website: 'The Internationlist 360')

And last but not least, here's my article about the Abraham Lincoln Brigade: [74] (More heroes.)

74) The Abraham Lincoln Brigade is the name given to Americans who volunteered to fight against Hitler, Mussolini, and Franco in the Spanish Civil War. 1986 marked the 50th anniversary of their historic effort.

Perspective of Lincoln Brigade : Heed the History of World Politics

The Sandinista government warmly welcomed the Abraham Lincoln Brigade delegation earlier this year, accepting with gratitude its donation of seven new ambulances now gleaming in the sun outside the reception room. Maury Colow, spokesman, shared the Brigade's sentiments with the Nicaraguans. "These seven ambulances are a symbol of our solidarity with your struggle. Your country's anguish is our anguish. It is a torment for us to witness the terrorism of our government, not our people. This is the response from those of us who cherish freedom and want Nicaragua to have freedom.

"Every damn country has the right to pick the kind of government they want. We witness the huge super-power trying to keep Nicaragua in its pocket, and we're reminded of Spain fighting Hitler and Mussolini."

Now Milt Wolff, who at twenty-three led some of the Lincoln Brigade's toughest battles against Franco's troops, adds to Maury's words. "We have been fighting fascism for fifty years now, and we promise you we will be doing it for fifty more — until you win your independence."

The delegation of twelve veterans, five wives, one widow, and two adult children represented the estimated three hundred fifty Brigade members still living in the U.S. To current generations, the Abraham Lincoln Brigade might sound like some new TV show. In fact, though, the battalion has been described as "the most heavily-fought and the most decorated group of men in the military history of the United States."

Herman Rosenstein — one of only ten Lincolns who fought the front line and was never wounded — is 71 now and lives in Santa Monica. In 1936, he was a 22-year-old bookkeeper at the William Morris Agency in New York City. Reading about the Spanish Civil War daily in the newspapers, and being Jewish, he was particularly sensitive to Hitler's activities.

"It just seemed to me," says Rosenstein now, "that Hitler could win in Spain. And Mussolini had already won in Ethiopia. Hitler had openly stated that he wanted to rule the world...why shouldn't he mean it?"

Spain was in an unusual and bloody situation. Franco's troops fought to overturn the elected government with tremendous aid from Mussolini and Hitler. (Hitler sent in the Condor Legion, consisting of 100 top fighters and bombers, 32 tanks, and 6,000 military men, while Mussolini sent ships with fully-equipped divisions of up to 100,000 men.)

Foreign *volunteers*, eventually numbering 40,000 from 52 countries, were in the hills and ditches beside the Spanish people, fighting to save the new democracy.

People like Herman Rosenstein felt that an elected government like the Spanish Republic (February of 1936) deserved a chance. He, therefore, joined an educational organization in New York called "The American League against War and Fascism."

One night, two of his friends from the organization — both a few years older than he — told him that they were going to Mexico. Rosenstein lay awake that night. It was the middle of the Depression; people simply didn't up and go to Mexico.

In fact, in the 1930s, people hardly traveled at all. Rosenstein himself hadn't been farther than New Jersey. It dawned on him that his friends were really going to Spain. Seeing them the next day, he said, "I wanna go to Mexico with you."

"No, no," they said, "you don't know what we're talking about."

"Yes, I do," said Rosenstein, "and I'm going, too."

It was illegal to go to Spain. U.S. passports were stamped: *Not valid for travel in Spain.* When Herman's passport arrived in the mail, his mother sent it straight back to Washington, to keep him from going to fight.

So Herman changed his last name to Klein, got another passport, and told his mother he was going to Cleveland to see his girl. He wrote a few letters in advance, about life in Cleveland, and arranged for the girl to periodically mail them to his mother.

Though concerned about Spain, the United States and Europe were at that time more concerned about their own well-being. Supposedly with the intention of separating Spain and its ugly problem from the rest of the world, the Non-intervention Agreement was signed by 27 nations, including the United States, France, Britain, Italy, and Germany.

A complete embargo against Spain, by all these nations, went into effect and kept the Spanish government from buying arms on the world market, as it was legally entitled to do. Yet, in spite of their agreements to the pact, Italy and Germany continued military aid to Franco.

Claude Bowers, the U.S. Ambassador to Spain from 1933 to 1939 called the Non-intervention Committee "...a shameless sham, cynically dishonest, in that Germany and Italy were consistently sending soldiers, planes, tanks, artillery, and ammunition into Spain without any interference or real protest from the signatories of the pact.... I wrote personally to Roosevelt that however good our intentions may have been at first, it had become quite clear that actually our embargo was operating powerfully for the benefit of the Axis."

The U.S. government, under Roosevelt, still allowed major corporations the right to extend credit to Franco. General Motors then supplied Franco with 14,000 trucks. Texaco sent over all the oil he required to run the war. And Dupont sent 60,000 aerial bombs.

In February 1938, a Gallup poll showed 76% of the American people in support of the Spanish Republic. Two years and millions of lives later, half the world was fighting Hitler and Mussolini in World War

II. Then Roosevelt told the Ambassador to Spain, "We made a mistake; you have been right all along."

The Spanish Civil War is now understood to have been the first battle of World War II.

A little office in New York City handled the logistics of getting tickets for Americans volunteering to fight in Spain. One way, since no one was expected to return. With their passage, the men were also given ten bucks and told that their other needs would be covered.

With his new identity and an invented destination, Rosenstein and his buddies boarded ship in June 1937, all carefully avoiding discussion about Spain during the voyage. But, upon disembarkation in France, a curiously large number of single male passengers headed for the same hotel, suspiciously non-tourist-like in appearance. They were all volunteers going to Spain.

In a restaurant that night, as they were served the first of many free meals to come, they saw that passion about the war was no secret in France. Many people there openly applauded the commitment of the international volunteers. As the Americans continued south toward Spain, people everywhere offered food and shelter, sometimes lining the streets in support.

From all over the world, contributions, donations, and volunteers arrived in Spain. From the United States, the Screen Actors Guild donated 2 ambulances; and Ernest Hemingway, single-handedly, raised money for 14, which were driven across the border from France. In Los Angeles, James Cagney, Gypsy Rose

Lee, Humphrey Bogart, and other celebrities openly backed the Spanish Republic.

Rosenstein and the others, each carrying one small parcel of personal belongings, crossed the Pyrenees Mountains between France and Spain. They traveled on foot, by night, for eleven and a half hours. Instead of lights, they used guide dogs at the front and rear of the line. Once inside Spain, buses and trains carried them inland to Albacete, the international base.

With no spare ammunition or supplies, training was in many cases non-existent. Large numbers of the Abraham Lincoln Brigade volunteers went directly into battle with no practice at loading or firing a rifle. Those that received instruction—Rosenstein was given 5 rounds to fire off before going into battle—had the same faulty, antique equipment as everyone else.

At the close of 1938, there were only 10,000 international volunteers left. The Americans, the youngest of the internationals, had lost 1000 men of the approximately 3200 that had gone over to fight. And 400 more Lincolns would lose their lives later in World War II.

Regarding Nicaragua, Rosenstein said, "The connections are so tight with us that we almost feel like we're in that war again." The Lincolns urgently wanted to offer tangible as well as moral support to Nicaragua, but coffee-picking was clearly not a consideration. The Brigade members wanted to create an involvement for all people, even the infirm, disabled, or medically restricted. So, in just over a year, $140,000 was raised for Sandinista ambulances. Now the shiny blue Toyota jeeps (the vehicles couldn't be American due to the U.S. embargo on Nicaragua), equipped for the roughest terrain or emergency, are there.

Maury Colow continued his address to the Nicaraguan government representatives, "We see so many parallels between Spain and Nicaragua. The people of Spain were brutally oppressed by absentee landlords and private business interests, just like the Nicaraguan people. They were hungry for land and liberty, just like the people here. General Anastasio Somoza, with the help of the United States, kept the people here oppressed, starved, and illiterate. To our shame, Ronald Reagan misuses our money, using a motley crew of mercenaries, gangsters, and former Somoza Guardsmen who bomb, rape, and murder. We see photos of destruction and misery that remind us of Spain. And we join you now in a familiar slogan that we used all the time in Spain, and is used all the time in Nicaragua…*No Pasaran!*"

Then former soldier, Bill Gandall said, "I was in the Marines in Nicaragua in 1928 and 1929. Our job was murder, rape, and the burning of villages, farms, and factories. The one man we were fighting against was Sandino. He was very clever. We never caught him. He was supported by the people.

"People of the United States need to know these things. They think the Marines were heroes. We were a bunch of bastards down here—young and stupid and brainwashed."

Wolff spoke again, "The 12 vets here today represent the 1000 comrades we left behind in the olive groves of Spain, as well as the 350 vets who couldn't come here. But I do not represent the policies of my president.

"This character in the White House compared the mercenaries (Contras) who are fighting against the Nicaraguan people to the struggle of the Abraham Lincoln Brigade in Spain. When he was reminded, like he must be reminded about so many things, that we were volunteers, not mercenaries, and fighting for the other side, he said, 'Oh. Well they fought on the wrong side.'

"Soon thereafter, Reagan made a trip to Spain to see Premier Gonzalez. There were 12,000 people in the street awaiting his arrival, with signs saying, 'We're all on the wrong side.'

"We know, from being down here in Nicaragua, that once again we are on President Reagan's wrong side. And damn glad about it."

— *The Easy Reader, May 1, 1986*
(and reprinted in several other U.S. papers)

~ End ~

Glossary ~ Spanish

Anastasio Somoza - *leader of Nicaragua's 45-year Somoza regime, overthrown finally by the Sandinistas in 1979*

Augusto Sandino - *acclaimed guerrilla warrior; skillfully led the Nicaraguan peasants' revolution in the 1920s and 1930s; Sandinistas are named after him*

barrios - *residential neighborhoods on the outskirts of cities; in N. America, the word may imply lower living standards*

brigadista - *a foreign volunteer on a work brigade supporting the Sandinista ideology in Nicaragua*

buenos noches - *good night*

calma - *calm, quiet; in reference to the war, means 'no fighting going on'*

campesinos - *countryfolk, farmers, peasants*

cervezas - *beers*

commandante - *commander, captain, usually a military leader*

compañeros - *companion, partner, co-worker, colleague, friend*

Contadora - *the name of an island off Panama,*

Contra / Contras - *U.S.-backed, armed rebels sent into Nicaragua to perpetrate guerrilla warfare against the Sandinista Government and Nicaraguan people*

desaparecidas - *means 'disappeared;' in Latin American wars, it pertained to people missing, or captured and taken by the enemy, never seen again (presumably killed)*

cordobas - *Nicaraguan currency*

documentos - *in this book, generally refers to official or government-issued identification papers—passports, work permits, visas, press credentials; also means simply 'documents'*

el frente - *the front; the beginning or front edge of a war zone; where the actual physical fighting starts*

fe - *faith; and has a political connotation in Nicaragua, too— faith in the Sandinista leadership*

frijoles - *beans*

FSLN - *official name of the Sandinista government—stands for 'Frente Sandinista de Liberacion Nacional' or 'Sandinista National Liberation Front'*
gallopinto - *rice and beans in combination*
gracias - *thank you*
gringo / gringa - *a non-Latino foreigner; in Central America, the word usually implies Caucasian and/ or North American origin or nationality*
guerrillas - *fighters engaging in covert warfare, usually rural, involving stealth, secrecy, hiding, ambush, camouflage, mines, espionage, deceit, and undercover operations*
hojada - *a tart, salty, white cheese*
hospedaje - *hostel or inexpensive motel*
internationalista - *someone in Nicaragua who's come from another country to support the Sandinista government*
interrogación - *interrogation*
la paz - *peace*
leche - *milk*
marcha - *a march, as in a peace march*
migración - *immigration*
Nicas - *colloquial term for Nicaraguans (Costa Ricans, btw, are 'Ticas')*
'No pasaran' - *they (the enemy) will not pass; they will not get past us; the Sandinista slogan during the Contra War*
Norteamerica - *North America; in relation to the Contra War, generally refers to the USA*
Norteamericano - *in this context, an American (male); 'Norteamericana' is a female, but technically could also be Canadian*
pasajeros - *passengers*

Glossary ~ Spanish ~ con't

periodistas - *people who work in media—journalists, filmmakers, videographers, photographers*

por favor - *please*

quien sabe? - *who knows?*

rancho - *hut, shanty, shack; may be a shelter along the road or trail for getting food and even overnight shelter; also means a farm or ranch*

refrescos - *fresh fruit drinks with added sugar*

refritos - *refried beans*

Sandinistas - *peasants and soldiers supporting the anti-Somoza revolution; loyal, idealistic followers of Augusto Sandino, the original guerrilla leader against Somoza*

señor - *sir, a man; or used to address someone, like "Mr."*

señora - *ma'am, a mature or married woman; or used to address someone, as in "Mrs." or "Ms."*

solidaridad - *solidarity*

solita - *alone (female), or solito (male); also 'sola' or 'solo'*

Somoza / Somoza regime - *Nicaragua's 45-year Somoza regime, originally led by Anastasio Somoza, then overthrown by the Sandinistas in 1979*

Somozas - *members of the Somoza family or the political party under the rule of the family; sometimes a name for followers of Somoza*

Somozistas - *official name for followers of the Somozas*

Sovietica - *Russian*

stupidos - *if you can't guess the meaning, then you are one*

todo - *all, everything*

Yanqui - *an American, i.e. a Yankee*

zona de guerra - *zone of war, war zone*

zona militar - *military zone; also usually means 'off-limits to all vehicles and persons except military,' or only those with military-approved documentation*

Glossary ~ English

Anastasio Somoza - *leader of Nicaragua's 45-year Somoza regime, overthrown finally by the Sandinistas in 1979*

bourgeoisie - *understood in Nicaragua as the moneyed class*

Contadora process - *a 1983 peace plan for Central America, called for by eight Latin American nations, attempting to end U.S. aggression towards Nicaragua, El Salvador, and Guatemala*

Contra / Contras - *U.S.-backed, armed rebels sent into Nicaragua to perpetrate guerrilla warfare against the Sandinista Government and Nicaraguan people*

covert - *clandestine, under cover; not openly acknowledged or displayed; possibly illegal*

FSLN - *official name of the Sandinista government—Sandinista National Liberation Front ('Frente Sandinista de Liberacion Nacional')*

guerrillas - *fighters engaging in covert warfare, usually rural, involving stealth, secrecy, hiding, ambush, camouflage, mines, espionage, deceit, and undercover operations*

imperialism - *extending the power and dominion of a nation by direct territorial acquisitions, or by gaining indirect control over the political or economic life of other territories or states*

populist - *of the people, by the people; a populist (people's) movement*

Sandinistas - *peasants and soldiers supporting the anti-Somoza revolution; loyal, idealistic followers of Augusto Sandino*

Sandino (Augusto) - *guerrilla warrior; successfully led the Nicaraguan peasants' revolution in the 1920s and 1930s; the Sandinistas are named after him*

Somozistas - *official name for followers of the Somozas*

Sullivan and Cromwell - *mega American law firm with powerful multi-national corporations as clients; asserted imperialistic muscle to manipulate and overthrow 'banana republics' in Central America and globally*

Yankee - *in Nicaragua, a Yankee is any American; may also be used derogatorily*

Bibliography

(not in particular order, because all the following sources have already been listed within the book)

~ The Christian Science Monitor, Oct. 26, 1984

~ "What Is a Banana Republic? Definition and Examples," by Longley, Robert, 'ThoughtCo,' Dec. 6, 2021, 'thoughtco.com/banana-republic-definition-4776041'

~ LA Weekly, August 15, 1986 & The LA Reader, May 12, 1986, "Architects and Planners Heads for Pancasan," by Wendy Raebeck

~ "The Nicaraguan Revolution: the Somoza Regime and Sandinistas," from 'study.com,' Jan. 22, 2015

~ "Sullivan and Cromwell: Capitalism, Intelligence, and Facism," interview with Hugo Turner, ('Our Hidden History.org')

~ "The United States' Involvement in Nicaragua," ("CourseHero.com")

~ "The Mouse Kills the Cat: Augusto Cesar Sandino's Rebellion against the US," by Daniel Kovalik, ('The Internationlist 360,' Feb. 21, 2022)

~ "The Bogotazo," by Jack Davis, July 2, 1996, CIA Historical Review Program (CIA.gov)

Bibliography ~ con't

~ "Miskitos and Sandinistas"
   by L. Proyect, <u>Columbia University</u> (no date given)

~ <u>The New Yorker</u>, September 23, 1996

~ <u>The Washington Post</u>, Opinion Section, March 28, 1982,
   "The Use and Abuse of the Miskito Indians" (no author named)

~ "<u>The Morning Call</u>," Lehigh Valley, PA newspaper, 12/27/87,
   "Troops a Part of Life in Honduras"

~ "<u>The Brothers—John Foster Dulles, Allen Dulles,
   and Their Secret World War</u>," book by Stephen Kinzer

~ <u>Courtesy Dept. of Defense, Still Media Records Center</u>,
   (data as of 1993)

~ "The Contra War in Nicaragua,"
   from the book, "<u>What Uncle Sam Really Wants</u>," 2002,
   by Noam Chomsky

~ "<u>Resistance and Contradiction: Miskito Indians and the
   Nicaraguan State, 1894-1987</u>," book by Charles R. Hale

~ <u>American University political scientist</u>, William M. LeoGrande

~ '<u>Splinter.com</u>'

~ "<u>Review of the World Situation as it Relates to the Security
   of the United States</u>" (article, May 12, 1948)

~ <u>The New York Times,</u> editorial, April 14, 1948

~ <u>Newsweek</u> – November 8, 1982

~ United Press International (<u>UPI.com</u>), Feb. 27, 1986

~ <u>The New York Times</u>, OpEd, August 8, 1986

~ "U.S. Gets Ready to Send G.I.'s to Train Contras,"
   <u>The New York Times,</u> August 21, 1986:

~ <u>LA Times</u>, October 14, 1986

~ <u>The Washington Post</u> – October 27, 1986

~ <u>LA Times</u>, November 13, 1986

~ <u>The New York Times</u>, December 18, 1986

~ <u>The New York Times</u>, December 31, 1986

~ The Cold War Experience, '<u>weebly.com</u>'

~ "<u>Presstitutes: Embedded in the Pay of the CIA:
   Confession from the Profession,</u>" **book** by Udo Ulfkotte

~ "Confession from the Profession: '<u>Presstitutes</u>' in the
   <u>Service of the CIA</u>, 11-19-2020, **article** by Tim Pelzer

~ "<u>The Science of Coercion</u>," book by Christopher Simpson

Bibliography ~ con't

~ "Monroe Doctrine," by <u>History.com</u> editors, 11-20-2021

~ <u>The Easy Reader</u>, "Broken," by Wendy Raebeck, Mar. 17, 1988
   (I had about 25 articles about Nicaragua published—can't list them all!)

~ "<u>At War with Nicaragua</u>," book by Richard Ullman
   (from "<u>CourseHero.com</u>")

~ "Why is the Nicaraguan Government Demonized by both
   Liberals and Conservatives when Nicaragua has seen
   Great Progress under the Sandinistas?"
      — by Stansfield Smith, March 28, 2022
         (from website: '<u>The Internationlist 360</u>')

~ Wikipedia - referenced for dates, a few sequences of
   events, and spelling of names, but not for comprehensive
   or controversial data

other books by W. M. Raebeck

"I Did Inhale — Memoir of a Hippie Chick"

"Expedition Costa Rica"

"Some Swamis are Fat" (under pen-name Ava Greene)

"Stars in Our Eyes — true stories"

"Silence of Islands — poems"

more books coming

audio versions of all books coming

VISIT 'WendyRaebeck.com'
~ sign onto my newsletter there ~
and receive free stories!

¡Y muchas, muchas gracias por su visita a Nicaragua conmigo!

No Pasaran

CPSIA information can be obtained
at www.ICGtesting.com
Printed in the USA
JSHW020213180722
28207JS00003B/17

9 781938 691188